ICEBOX CAKES

RECIPES FOR *the* COOLEST CAKES IN TOWN

JEAN SAGENDORPH AND JESSIE SHEEHAN

PHOTOGRAPHS BY TARA DONNE

CHRONICLE BOOKS

SAN FRANCISCO

Text copyright © 2015 by Jean Sagendorph and Jessie Sheehan.
Photographs copyright © 2015 by Tara Donne.

Library of Congress Cataloging-in-Publication Data available.
ISBN 978-1-4521-1221-3

Manufactured in China

Designed by **ANNE KENADY**
Food styling by **CHELSEA ZIMMER**
Typesetting by **HOWIE SEVERSON**

10 9 8 7 6 5 4 3 2

Chronicle Books LLC
680 Second Street
San Francisco, California 94107
www.chroniclebooks.com

JEAN:
FOR MOMENDORPH

JESSIE:
**FOR OLIVER
AND JACK**

CONTENTS

WHAT IS AN ICEBOX CAKE?

what

IS AN

ICEBOX CAKE?

IN AMERICAN HOMES OF THE 1950S, IT WAS THE DARLING OF THE DESSERT TABLE—LAYERS OF CHOCOLATE WAFERS AND WHIPPED CREAM ENROBED IN MORE WHIPPED CREAM, THAT, AFTER A SPELL IN THE REFRIGERATOR, MAGICALLY MELDED INTO SOMETHING THAT WAS CREAMY AND WONDERFULLY CAKEY. YOU MIGHT NOT HAVE KNOWN IT WAS CALLED AN ICEBOX CAKE— YOU JUST KNEW IT TASTED LIKE A DREAM, AND YOU WANTED MORE.

Icebox cakes did not spring full-blown from mid-century American kitchens. Instead, the cakes evolved from Marie-Antoine Carême's French *charlotte*—a luscious chilled and molded dessert of ladyfingers and custards popular a century before. Carême is considered the father of French cuisine and, in our opinion, also of the icebox cake. His Charlottes à la Parisienne or à la Russe are well documented in his 1815 cookbook *The Royal Parisian Pastry Cook and Confectioner*.

In the 1920s, the National Biscuit Company (now known as Nabisco) put their Famous Chocolate Wafers on the market and included a recipe for an icebox cake on the packaging. Housewives began layering the wafers with whipped cream and placing them in their iceboxes to set up. No oven was required and a delicious step toward convenience was taken.

Driven by her obsession with whipped cream, Jean came across a recipe for an icebox cake and fell in love. She experimented a little, using store-bought ingredients and her own fillings. She decided to share the love, serving them to friends and posting pictures on her blog and on Facebook. When her results garnered praise—"THIS IS THE GREATEST THING I'VE EVER EATEN!"—she knew she was on to something.

Recognizing a tasty opportunity, Jean started working on this cookbook, but she knew she would need a partner in crime to fully attack the flavor spectrum. A friend suggested that she reach out to Jessie. They made plans to meet up for tea (and cake!) and instantly hit it off.

Jessie has always loved homey desserts—a favorite is her grandmother's lemon velvet cake, replicated herein as the Luscious Lemon (page 112)—so when Jean suggested that she and Jessie write a cookbook about icebox cakes, Jessie was totally on board.

In this book, you will find Jean's and Jessie's favorite icebox cake recipes, and we hope that you'll make many of the cakes. We're pretty sure you will be rewarded with a big smile and a hug. An icebox cake is really a simple dessert that can be playfully fun or decadently sophisticated. The choice is truly yours. So roll up your sleeves and prepare to wield your whisk.

CH. **1**

BEFORE

—— YOU ——

BEGIN

TOOLS

WE UNDERSTAND THAT NOT EVERY KITCHEN IS OUTFITTED WITH FANCY COOKING UTENSILS AND APPLIANCES. JEAN JUST PICKED UP HER FIRST STAND MIXER A FEW YEARS AGO—A TOTAL SCORE AT A THRIFT STORE (TALK ABOUT LUCKY!). SO DON'T WORRY— YOU WILL BE ABLE TO MAKE ALL OF THE RECIPES IN THIS BOOK USING ITEMS ROUTINELY FOUND IN A BASIC KITCHEN ARSENAL.

BAKING PANS

An 8-by-8-by-2-in/20-by-20-by-5-cm baking pan (metal or glass) makes the perfect-size cake for a small party (and is the pan we use for smaller cakes); a 9-by-13-by-2-in/23-by-33-by-5-cm rectangular baking pan (metal or glass) creates an ideal icebox cake for a crowd. That is what we use when making the Salty Milk Dud (the sides of the pan contain the ooziness of the combo of caramel and pudding). A 9-by-5-by-3-in/23-by-12-by-7.5-cm loaf pan (metal or glass) makes a comparable-sized cake to the 8-in/20-cm square, but with a slightly more unique presentation: This cake can be popped from the pan before serving to showcase all of its lovely layers.

BAKING SHEETS

For baking wafers, graham crackers, and ladyfingers, the default pan is a standard-size, heavy-duty, rimmed baking sheet (also called a half sheet pan), typically about 18 by 13 in/46 by 33 cm. Using two baking sheets is most efficient. Have one sheet prepped and waiting for the oven while your wafers or other baked goods are baking on the other.

CANDY THERMOMETER

You will need a candy thermometer (also known as a deep-frying thermometer) for making Marshmallow-Cream Whipped Cream (page 72). The thermometer tracks the rising temperature of the hot syrup. At just the right stage, the syrup is removed from the heat and mixed with beaten egg whites, and the two magically transform into a deliciously fluffy marshmallow cream.

ELECTRIC MIXER

If you bake a lot, a stand mixer is a good investment for its capacity and muscle. That said, a hand mixer will work just fine for these recipes.

FOOD PROCESSOR

Clearly your great-grandmother did not have a food processor, but chances are you do. The Pistachio-Chocolate (page 32) is the only recipe that requires one.

GRATER/ZESTER

A Microplane or other fine grater is best for zesting lemons, oranges, and limes. It does a great job removing just the colored zest (a carrier of flavorful oils), leaving the bitter white pith behind. In a pinch, you can use a paring knife or vegetable peeler to remove ribbons of zest, which you then finely chop. You can also use a peeler to shave chocolate over a finished cake.

KITCHEN SCALE

Professional bakers weigh ingredients for the most precise and consistent results. When we fill a cup of flour, for instance, we use the scoop and sweep method: We plunge our measuring cup into our bag of flour, scooping the flour so that when we lift up the cup, excess flour extends over its rim. We then use the flat side of a knife to sweep off the excess flour. With this method, 1 cup of flour weighs 4¾ oz/135 g. However, if a different baker used the spoon and sweep method (spooning flour into the cup, rather than plunging and scooping it), the cup of flour would weigh less than 4¾ oz/135 g. If you weigh your ingredients, there is no need to know the method used to fill a cup of flour: You'll automatically add the same amount every time you make the recipe.

KNIVES

Use a chef's knife (we prefer one with an 8-in/20-cm blade) to cut your logs of wafer dough or blocks of graham cracker dough into thin slices. Use a paring knife to help release a cake from a springform pan by loosening its edges from the sides of the pan.

MEASURING CUPS

A set of accurate measuring cups—a must-have in every kitchen—helps ensure a recipe's success. You'll want a set of individual cups for dry ingredients and a measuring pitcher for liquids. Dry measuring cups do not reflect true volume measurements, and as such do not correspond to liquid measures. A standard set of dry measuring cups should include ¼-cup/60-ml, ⅓-cup/75-ml, ½-cup/125-ml, and 1-cup/250-ml scoops. A clear measuring cup for liquids, showing standard (ounces and cups) and metric (millilitres) amounts, has a spout that directs your liquids cleanly into your mixing bowl.

MEASURING SPOONS

Measuring spoons will aid you in adding just the right small amount of an ingredient. A standard five-piece set should include ⅛-teaspoon, ¼-teaspoon, ½-teaspoon, 1-teaspoon, and 1-tablespoon sizes.

MIXING BOWLS

If Jean had her way, she would own dozens of sets of mixing bowls. (She covets her grandmother's set, of which her sister has custody.) They're a personal passion of hers. Pick a set that is functional—large-bottomed and sturdy—in graduated sizes, and preferably nesting for compact storage. Also choose bowls that are aesthetically pleasing to you, since you'll have them for a long time. Jean's day-to-day set is vintage Pyrex in the Butterprint Amish pattern. Using these bowls makes her happy, but they aren't so dear that she can't bang them around. Jessie prefers simple metal mixing bowls, ideally with rubber bottoms (so they don't slide around on the counter), and in three graduated sizes, 5 qt/4.5 L, 8 qt/7.5 L, and 13 qt/12 L.

PARCHMENT PAPER

Lining baking sheets and pans with parchment paper allows baked goods to release with ease, makes cleanup a snap, and keeps your pans in tip-top shape. Line the sides of a springform pan with parchment to protect the layers of the cake.

PASTRY BAG

To shape ladyfingers, you pipe thin fingers of batter onto a baking sheet. Traditionally, they're piped through a pastry bag with a decorative tip (we use a ½-in/12-mm #806 Ateco round tip). You'll find pastry bags made of canvas, plastic, or disposable polyethylene, plus interchangeable stainless-steel tips. That said, a heavy-duty, resealable plastic bag will work in a pinch. Simply fill a large plastic bag with your batter and snip off a small piece of one corner to create a piping hole. Squeeze the bag gently and begin piping. You can play around with the size of the hole (but be sure to start small) until you find a size that will pipe a ladyfinger that's about 3 by 1 in/7.5 by 2.5 cm.

PLASTIC WRAP

For an icebox cake assembled in a loaf pan, plastic wrap is essential for easy removal of the finished cake. Plastic wrap is also necessary to wrap your cake—no matter its size—while it sets up during its requisite stint in the refrigerator. Finally, if you're freezing an icebox cake to enjoy at a later date, do so by placing it in the freezer unwrapped until frozen, then wrap it in plastic wrap and return it to the freezer for up to 1 month.

SIEVE

For removing lumpy bits from dry ingredients like cocoa powder or ground ginger; trapping seeds from fruit in a purée; or smoothing out pudding or lemon curd, you need a medium-mesh wire sieve.

Use a wooden spoon, rubber spatula, or whisk to press the pudding, curd, or purée through the sieve. A sieve is also useful for dusting a cake with cocoa powder, cinnamon, or confectioners' sugar.

SPATULAS

You'll want a metal or stiff plastic spatula to transfer baked goods from baking sheet to cooling rack. It's also useful for flattening your wafers and graham crackers upon removal from the oven. An offset spatula, with an angled neck that allows the blade to more easily slide under baked goods, is a bit thinner than a regular spatula and is perfect for removing just-baked ladyfingers from a baking sheet. You can also use it to spread pudding, whipped cream, caramel, and ganache. You'll find rubber or silicone spatulas with flexible, heatproof blades are a big help in the kitchen. Use one to easily scrape out every last bit of whipped cream, pudding, peanut butter, ganache, etc. from a mixing bowl.

SPRINGFORM PAN

If you don't have a round 9-by-3-in/23-by-7.5-cm springform pan, here's a great excuse to pick one up. A nonstick version is unnecessary for an icebox cake, but is a nice feature when using it to bake other desserts. A springform is a great option for large icebox cakes and produces an extremely pretty dessert. The springform pan sides release from the bottom by opening a clamp, making it easy to remove baked goods in one piece.

WHISK

This essential tool is used to blend and incorporate air into ingredients. If you don't already have a whisk, consider adding a medium metal whisk in a teardrop shape (not balloon shape) to your collection of kitchen utensils.

ICEBOX LAYERS

THE WAFER, GRAHAM CRACKER, AND LADYFINGER LAYERS

When layered with whipped cream or pudding and left to sit in the refrigerator for several hours, the wafers, graham crackers, or ladyfingers of an icebox cake will soften to an almost cakelike texture. The best wafers and graham crackers for an icebox cake are thin, dry, and crisp, and the best ladyfingers are delicately spongy with a slightly crusty exterior.

If you are not keen on making cookies from scratch, do not fret. You can make every cake in this book by preparing homemade whipped cream or pudding and purchasing store-bought wafers, crackers, and ladyfingers. See Store-Bought Cookies: Our Favorites (page 16) for a list of our recommendations. Just make sure you choose a store-bought cookie that shares some of the features of our homemade ones.

THE CREAMY LAYERS

The whipped cream or pudding layer of your icebox cake is the one magically absorbed by your cookie, and the one that transforms your wafer, cracker, or ladyfinger from something crispy, dry, or spongy into something downright soft and pillowy.

STORE-BOUGHT COOKIES: THE STINT IN THE FRIDGE

Cakes made with store-bought cookies set up in much less time in the refrigerator (5 to 8 hours) than cakes made with homemade cookies (about 24 hours).

MAKING AHEAD, FREEZING, LEFTOVERS

If making your icebox cake ahead of time, after the requisite stint in the fridge, you may keep your cake refrigerated for an additional 24 hours before serving it. Decorate it just prior to serving.

If you would like to freeze your loaf or spring-form cake for future use, you may do so after its required time in the fridge. With a loaf pan, pop the cake from the pan, remove the plastic wrap, and freeze. Once fully frozen, wrap it in plastic wrap and return it to the freezer for up to 1 month. With a springform pan, you'll do best if you line the bottom of the pan with plastic wrap before you begin assembling the cake. To begin the freezing process, you'll need to remove the sides of the pan from the cake and then place it in the freezer, unwrapped, until it's frozen. Once fully frozen, remove the bottom of the pan, wrap the cake in plastic wrap, and return it to the freezer for up to 1 month. Cakes assembled in square and rectangular baking pans can be wrapped without any prefreezing preparation. Thaw frozen cakes in the refrigerator for at least 8 hours before decorating and serving.

Leftover icebox cakes should be covered, then stored in the refrigerator and enjoyed within 48 hours.

DECORATING ICEBOX CAKES

Once you have assembled your cake, it's time to think about decorating it. Here are some ideas to play around with:

- Lightly dust on cinnamon (or a mixture of cinnamon and granulated sugar), cocoa powder, confectioners' sugar, cayenne pepper (for pepper-friendly flavors as in the Mexican Chocolate Spice cake on page 28), or any other sugar or spice that will complement the ingredients of your cake.

- Crumble, crush, or chop graham crackers, wafers, nuts, chocolate-covered espresso beans, Whoppers, chocolate-covered peppermint candies, candy canes, peanut butter cups, or lemon hard candies and scatter them on top.

- Place small candies (such as Whoppers, Junior Mints, mini peanut butter cups, Milk Duds, or Red Hots), mini chocolate chips or callets, or mini marshmallows around the perimeter of the cake.

- Drizzle raspberry purée, salty caramel, or ganache over the top.

- Sprinkle on fresh berries, flaky sea salt, colored sugar, Sugar In the Raw, finishing sugar, nonpareils, chocolate nibs, chocolate jimmies, shaved chocolate, and such.

- Tint any extra whipped cream with an appropriate shade of food coloring and pipe it into rosettes on top of the cake.

STORE-BOUGHT COOKIES:

our

FAVORITES

These are the specific brands of cookies and graham crackers that we buy for the cakey layers of our icebox cakes when we might not have time to bake. If you can't find them, your supermarket will surely stock good substitutes. Our list includes cookies in the same flavors as our homemade ones and of the same crispy, thin variety. For graham crackers, we mention our favorite (flavorwise), but any graham cracker will do. Ladyfingers are a bit trickier, as we haven't yet found a brand we like that is widely available. When looking for ladyfingers, choose soft, cakey ones as opposed to super-crispy, and look for them in specialty stores that carry Italian foods.

Nabisco Famous Chocolate Wafers These cookies are very thin and dry, and perfect in an icebox cake, as they absorb the whipped cream quickly and turn cakey in only a matter of hours. Rumor has it that they can be hard to find, but we've discovered that most grocery store chains do carry them in the cookie section, or you can always order them online. Each box contains about 45 cookies, enough to make a log-shaped cake or a small cake in an 8-by-8-in/20-by-20-cm pan or a 9-by-5-in/23-by-12-cm loaf pan. The cookies are 2¼ in/5.5 cm in diameter, and we recommend making our homemade wafers the same size.

Nabisco Nilla Wafers or Keebler Vanilla Wafers Both of these wafers are a good base for cakes with very flavorful fillings since, like a blank slate, they assume the overall flavor of the filling quite nicely. These cookies are much smaller than Nabisco's Chocolate Wafers (and our homemade version).

16

Nabisco Grahams Original Crackers, Traditional and Chocolate We love the flavor of this cracker (easily found in the cookie aisle of your local grocery store), but really any graham cracker will do. Graham crackers tend to come in the shape of a 2½-by-5-in/6-by-12-cm rectangle. If graham crackers are not available, digestive biscuits, although a different shape, are a good substitute.

Trader Joe's Meyer Lemon Cookie Thins If you happen to be lucky enough to live near a Trader Joe's, these cookies are fantastic. They are wonderfully thin and crispy (ideal for absorbing whipped cream and becoming cakey) and yet bursting with lemony flavor.

Back to Nature's California Lemon Cookie This is a good, crisp lemon cookie. Not quite as thin as Trader Joe's cookie, but equally flavorful.

Anna's Thins Anna's offers ginger thins and chocolate mint thins, among other flavors.

17

CH. 2

the

RECIPES

OUR CAKES RUN THE GAMUT, FROM THOSE
INSPIRED BY YOUR FAVORITE HALLOWEEN
CANDY AND CAMPFIRE TREAT TO THOSE WITH
SOPHISTICATED FLAVOR PROFILES LIKE THE LEMON-
CARAMEL, BLACK PEPPER–RUM, AND LAVENDER-
BLUEBERRY CAKES. NONE OF THE RECIPES IS
TERRIBLY COMPLICATED, BUT SOME DEMAND JUST
A BIT MORE LABOR THAN OTHERS—AND ALL WILL
PRODUCE THE TASTIEST CAKES IMAGINABLE.

OLD SCHOOL

YIELD: 9 TO 12 SERVINGS

This cake—aptly named Old School—is adapted from Nabisco's original icebox cake recipe from the 1930s. It is the simplest and, arguably, one of the tastiest icebox cakes around, and is the perfect balance of chocolate and vanilla. We think it tastes like the world's most exquisite Oreo cookie. (You'll have extra wafers left over after assembling your cake—lucky you! Store them in a resealable plastic bag in the freezer and enjoy them for up to 1 month.)

One 10-in/25-cm oval or rectangular serving platter

CHOCOLATE WAFERS

MAKES ABOUT SIXTY
2¼-IN/5.5-CM WAFERS

1¼ cups/170 g all-purpose flour

¾ cup/75 g Dutch-process cocoa powder

½ tsp salt

1¼ cups/250 g granulated sugar

¾ cup/170 g unsalted butter, at room temperature

2 tsp pure vanilla extract

2 Tbsp whole milk

1 Tbsp light corn syrup

VANILLA WHIPPED CREAM

MAKES ABOUT 6 CUPS/720 G

3 cups/720 ml heavy cream

⅓ cup/45 g confectioners' sugar

1½ tsp pure vanilla extract

Chocolate shavings for decorating

→

MAKE *the* WAFERS

In a medium bowl, whisk together the flour, cocoa powder, and salt.

In the bowl of a stand mixer fitted with the paddle attachment, cream the granulated sugar, butter, and vanilla on medium-low speed until slightly fluffy, about 2 minutes. Be careful not to overbeat. Scrape the sides of the bowl with a rubber spatula.

In a small bowl, whisk the milk and corn syrup to combine. Add the milk mixture to the butter-sugar mixture with the mixer on medium-low speed; beat until just combined. Scrape the sides of the bowl with the rubber spatula.

Add the flour mixture all at once to the mixer bowl. With the mixer on low speed, beat until the dough just begins to pull away from the bottom of the bowl and forms a cohesive mass. Scrape the sides of the bowl to fully incorporate all the ingredients.

Divide the dough in half and place each half on a sheet of plastic wrap. Loosely wrap the dough and form each half into a log about 2 in/5 cm wide. Roll the logs along the counter, still wrapped in plastic wrap, in order to shape into perfect cylinders. Tighten the plastic wrap around the logs and freeze them for at least 2 hours, or overnight. If you have trouble forming the soft dough into logs, form the dough into a disk (or loose log shape), wrap it in plastic wrap, and place in the freezer for about 20 minutes, just until it is cold enough to shape into the necessary log. Line two baking sheets with parchment paper.

Once frozen, unwrap one of the logs and use a sharp paring or chef's knife to cut it into thin slices about ⅛ in/3 mm thick; rotate the log as you slice, or the side sitting on the cutting surface will flatten. Arrange the slices about 1 in/2.5 cm apart on one of the prepared baking sheets and place in the freezer for at least 10 minutes. Repeat with the second dough log and prepared baking sheet. If you need more room to fit all your dough slices, simply arrange them on additional sheets of parchment paper, layer the dough-covered papers one on top of the other on the second baking sheet in the freezer, and switch them out as you bake off each batch. (You can also wrap the baking sheets in plastic wrap and freeze the rounds for up to 1 week.)

Position a rack in the center of the oven and preheat to 350°F/180°C.

Place one baking sheet of frozen dough rounds in the oven and bake until they appear dry, 10 to 12 minutes, rotating the sheet halfway through the baking time. Using a stiff metal or plastic spatula, immediately press down lightly on each cookie to flatten it. Let the wafers cool on the baking sheet for 2 to 3 minutes, then transfer them to a wire rack to cool completely. The wafers should be very crispy when cooled. If they are not, place them back in the 350°F/180°C oven for 1 to 2 minutes more. Repeat to bake the additional sheets of frozen dough rounds.

Store the wafers in an airtight container as soon as they have cooled. They will remain crispy at room temperature, tightly sealed, for about 24 hours. Freezing the baked wafers in a resealable plastic bag also works well, for up to 1 month. There is no need to defrost the wafers before assembling your cake.

———————

MAKE *the* WHIPPED CREAM

Refrigerate the bowl of a stand mixer and the whisk attachment (or a medium metal bowl and beaters from a hand mixer) until quite cold, about 15 minutes.

Once chilled, remove the bowl and whisk from the refrigerator, add the cream, and whip it on medium speed until just thickened.

Add the confectioners' sugar and vanilla and, on medium-high speed, whip the cream until it holds stiff peaks that stand upright when the whisk is raised (the stiffer the cream, the more support it will provide the wafers in your cake). Use it immediately.

———————

Have the serving platter ready. Using a small spatula or butter knife, spread about 1 Tbsp of the whipped cream on the domed (top) side of eight of the wafers. Stack the coated wafers, and then set them aside. Repeat with the remaining wafers until you have five stacks of eight wafers each. You may want fewer layers depending on the thickness of your wafers.

On the platter, carefully place the stacks on their sides and gently press them together end to end, forming a log. Cover the entire log with a thick layer of the whipped cream. Gently cover the cake with plastic wrap. Refrigerate for 24 hours.

Peel the plastic wrap from the cake and decorate the top of the cake with chocolate shavings. Serve it directly from the platter, using a knife to cut the cake into slices diagonally.

PEPPERMINT-CHOCOLATE

YIELD: 15 TO 20 SERVINGS

This cake is an ode to York Peppermint Patties, Andes Mints (swiped from your grandmother's candy bowl), and mint–chocolate chip ice cream.

One 9-by-3-in/23-by-7.5-cm springform pan

CHOCOLATE-PEPPERMINT WAFERS

MAKES ABOUT SIXTY 2¼-IN/5.5-CM WAFERS

1¼ cups/170 g all-purpose flour

¾ cup/75 g Dutch-process cocoa powder

½ tsp salt

1¼ cups/250 g granulated sugar

¾ cup/170 g unsalted butter, at room temperature

2 Tbsp peppermint extract

2 Tbsp whole milk

1 Tbsp light corn syrup

DARK CHOCOLATE–PEPPERMINT GANACHE

MAKES ABOUT 2 CUPS/610 G

13 oz/370 g dark chocolate (60 to 70 percent cacao), finely chopped

A generous 1¼ cups/300 ml heavy cream

1 tsp peppermint extract, or to taste

PEPPERMINT WHIPPED CREAM

MAKES ABOUT 8 CUPS/1 KG

1 qt/960 ml heavy cream

½ cup/65 g confectioners' sugar

¼ cup/60 ml crème de menthe

1 tsp peppermint extract

4 to 5 drops green food coloring (optional)

Chopped chocolate candies with creamy peppermint fillings for decorating

MAKE the WAFERS

In a medium bowl, whisk together the flour, cocoa powder, and salt.

In the bowl of a stand mixer fitted with the paddle attachment, cream the granulated sugar, butter, and peppermint extract on medium-low speed until slightly fluffy, about 2 minutes. Be careful not to overbeat. Scrape the sides of the bowl with a rubber spatula.

In a small bowl, whisk the milk and corn syrup to combine. Add the milk mixture to the butter-sugar mixture with the mixer on medium-low speed; beat until just combined. Scrape the sides of the bowl with the rubber spatula.

Add the flour mixture all at once to the mixer bowl. With the mixer on low speed, beat until the dough just begins to pull away from the bottom of the bowl and forms a cohesive mass. Scrape the sides of the bowl to fully incorporate all the ingredients.

Divide the dough in half and place each half on a sheet of plastic wrap. Loosely wrap the dough and form each half into a log about 2 in/5 cm wide. Roll the logs along the counter, still wrapped in plastic wrap, in order to shape into perfect cylinders. Tighten the plastic wrap around the logs and freeze them for at least 2 hours, or overnight. If you have trouble forming the soft dough into logs, form the dough into a disk (or loose log shape), wrap it in plastic wrap, and place in the freezer for about 20 minutes, just until it is cold enough to shape into the necessary log. Line two baking sheets with parchment paper.

Once frozen, unwrap one of the logs and use a sharp paring or chef's knife to cut it into thin slices about 1/8 in/3 mm thick; rotate the log as you slice, or the side sitting on the cutting surface will flatten. Arrange the slices about 1 in/2.5 cm apart on one of the prepared baking sheets and place in the freezer for at least 10 minutes. Repeat with the second dough log and prepared baking sheet. If you need more room to fit all your dough slices, simply arrange them on additional sheets of parchment paper, layer the dough-covered papers one on top of the other on the second baking sheet in the freezer, and switch them out as you bake off each batch. (You can also wrap the baking sheets in plastic wrap and freeze the rounds for up to 1 week.)

Position a rack in the center of the oven and preheat to 350°F/180°C.

Place one baking sheet of the frozen dough rounds in the oven and bake until they appear dry, 10 to 12 minutes, rotating the sheet halfway through the baking time. Using a stiff metal or plastic spatula, immediately press down lightly on each cookie to flatten it. Let the wafers cool on the baking sheet for 2 to 3 minutes, then transfer them to a wire rack to cool completely. The wafers should be very crispy when cooled. If they are not, place them back in the 350°F/180°C oven for 1 to 2 minutes more. Repeat to bake the additional sheets of frozen dough rounds.

Store the wafers in an airtight container as soon as they have cooled. They will remain crispy at room temperature, tightly sealed, for about 24 hours. Freezing the baked wafers in a resealable plastic bag also works well, for up to

1 month. There is no need to defrost the wafers before assembling your cake.

MAKE *the* GANACHE

Place the chocolate in a medium heatproof bowl and set aside. In a small saucepan, heat the cream over medium-high heat just until bubbles begin to form around the edges.

Pour the warm cream over the chocolate and let sit for 1 minute so it begins to melt. Gently whisk until fully incorporated and shiny. Add the peppermint extract and whisk again.

Let come to room temperature, stirring occasionally, until it thickens and is less like chocolate syrup and pours more like hot fudge.

(To make ahead, let cool to room temperature, cover, and refrigerate for up to 1 week. Reheat over medium-low heat until liquefied.)

MAKE *the* WHIPPED CREAM

Refrigerate the bowl of a stand mixer and the whisk attachment (or a medium metal bowl and beaters from a hand mixer) until quite cold, about 15 minutes.

Once chilled, remove the bowl and whisk from the refrigerator, add the cream, and whip it on medium speed until just thickened.

Add the confectioners' sugar, crème de menthe, peppermint extract, and food coloring (if using) and, on medium-high speed, whip the cream until it holds stiff peaks that stand upright when the whisk is raised (the stiffer the cream, the more support it will provide the wafers in your cake). Use it immediately.

Lightly coat the sides of your springform pan with cooking spray and line the sides of the pan with a 3-by-29-in/7.5-by-75-cm strip of parchment paper. Using a small offset spatula or the back of a spoon, spread a generous layer of the whipped cream on the bottom of the pan.

Cover as much of the whipped cream as possible with a layer of the wafers, filling any gaps with broken wafers. The pieces should touch. The goal is a solid layer of wafers.

Generously spread a layer of the ganache over the wafers.

Continue layering in this order (whipped cream, wafers, ganache) until you run out or reach the top of the pan. Spread the top of the cake with a final layer of the whipped cream and gently cover it with plastic wrap. Refrigerate for 24 hours.

Peel the plastic wrap from the cake and run a paring knife between the paper and the pan. Open the clamp, remove the pan sides, and gently peel back the parchment paper. Transfer the cake, still on the pan bottom, to a serving platter. Place the candies around the edge of the cake. Using a knife, slice into wedges and serve.

MEXICAN CHOCOLATE SPICE

YIELD: 12 TO 15 SERVINGS

This cake is for those who like a little heat with their chocolate. The combination of cinnamon, black pepper, chili powder, and just a touch of cayenne gives this cake an unexpected kick. (You'll have extra wafers left over after assembling your cake—lucky you! Store them in a resealable plastic bag in the freezer and enjoy them for up to 1 month.)

One 9-by-5-by-3-in/23-by-12-by-7.5-cm loaf pan

One 10-in/25-cm oval or rectangular serving platter

MEXICAN CHOCOLATE SPICE WAFERS

MAKES ABOUT SIXTY
2¼-IN/5.5-CM WAFERS

1¼ cups/170 g all-purpose flour

¾ cup/75 g Dutch-process cocoa powder

1 Tbsp ground cinnamon

1 tsp chili powder

½ tsp freshly ground black pepper

¾ tsp salt

1¼ cups/250 g granulated sugar

¾ cup/170 g unsalted butter, at room temperature

2 tsp pure vanilla extract

2 Tbsp whole milk

1 Tbsp light corn syrup

SPICY WHIPPED CREAM

MAKES ABOUT 6 CUPS/720 G

3 cups/720 ml heavy cream

⅓ cup/45 g confectioners' sugar

2 tsp pure vanilla extract

1½ tsp ground cinnamon

¼ to ½ tsp cayenne pepper

Ground cinnamon and granulated sugar, whisked together until well blended, for decorating

28

→

MAKE *the* WAFERS

In a medium bowl, whisk together the flour, cocoa powder, spices, and salt.

In the bowl of a stand mixer fitted with the paddle attachment, cream the granulated sugar, butter, and vanilla on medium-low speed until slightly fluffy, about 2 minutes. Be careful not to overbeat. Scrape the sides of the bowl with a rubber spatula.

In a small bowl, whisk the milk and corn syrup to combine. Add the milk mixture to the butter-sugar mixture with the mixer on medium-low speed; beat until just combined. Scrape the sides of the bowl with the rubber spatula.

Add the flour mixture all at once to the mixer bowl. With the mixer on low speed, beat until the dough just begins to pull away from the bottom of the bowl and forms a cohesive mass. Scrape the sides of the bowl to fully incorporate all the ingredients.

Divide the dough in half and place each half on a sheet of plastic wrap. Loosely wrap the dough and form each half into a log about 2 in/5 cm wide. Roll the logs along the counter, still wrapped in plastic wrap, in order to shape into perfect cylinders. Tighten the plastic wrap around the logs and freeze them for at least 2 hours, or overnight. If you have trouble forming the soft dough into logs, form the dough into a disk (or loose log shape), wrap it in plastic wrap, and place in the freezer for about 20 minutes, just until it is cold enough to shape into the necessary log. Line two baking sheets with parchment paper.

Once frozen, unwrap one of the logs and use a sharp paring or chef's knife to cut it into thin slices about ⅛ in/3 mm thick; rotate the log as you slice, or the side sitting on the cutting surface will flatten. Arrange the slices about 1 in/2.5 cm apart on one of the prepared baking sheets and place in the freezer for at least 10 minutes. Repeat with the second dough log and prepared baking sheet. If you need more room to fit all your dough slices, simply arrange them on additional sheets of parchment paper, layer the dough-covered papers one on top of the other on the second baking sheet in the freezer, and switch them out as you bake off each batch. (You can also wrap the baking sheets in plastic wrap and freeze the rounds for up to 1 week.)

Position a rack in the center of the oven and preheat to 350°F/180°C.

Place one baking sheet of the frozen dough rounds in the oven and bake until they appear dry, 10 to 12 minutes, rotating the sheet halfway through the baking time. Using a stiff metal or plastic spatula, immediately press down lightly on each cookie to flatten it. Let the wafers cool on the baking sheet for 2 to 3 minutes, then transfer them to a wire rack to cool completely. The wafers should be very crispy when cooled. If they are not, place them back in the 350°F/180°C oven for 1 to 2 minutes more. Repeat to bake the additional sheets of frozen dough rounds.

Store the wafers in an airtight container as soon as they have cooled. They will remain crispy at room temperature, tightly sealed, for about 24 hours. Freezing the baked wafers in a resealable plastic bag also works well, for up to 1 month. There is no need to defrost the wafers before assembling your cake.

MAKE *the* WHIPPED CREAM

Refrigerate the bowl of a stand mixer and the whisk attachment (or a medium metal bowl and beaters from a hand mixer) until quite cold, about 15 minutes.

Once chilled, remove the bowl and whisk from the refrigerator, add the cream, and whip it on medium speed until just thickened.

Add the confectioners' sugar, vanilla, cinnamon, and cayenne and, on medium-high speed, whip the cream until it holds stiff peaks that stand upright when the whisk is raised (the stiffer the cream, the more support it will provide the wafers in your cake). Use it immediately.

Line the loaf pan with plastic wrap that hangs slightly over the pan sides. Using a small offset spatula or the back of a spoon, spread a generous layer of the whipped cream on the bottom of the lined pan.

Cover as much of the whipped cream as possible with a layer of the wafers, filling any gaps with broken wafers. The pieces should touch. The goal is a solid layer of wafers.

Continue layering whipped cream and wafers until you run out or reach the top of the pan, ending with whipped cream. Gently cover the cake with plastic wrap. Refrigerate for 24 hours.

Peel the plastic wrap from the cake, place the serving platter over the cake, and invert the cake onto the platter. Carefully remove the pan and plastic-wrap lining and dust the cinnamon sugar on top of the cake. Using a knife, cut it into slices and serve.

PISTACHIO-CHOCOLATE

YIELD: 12 TO 15 SERVINGS

Pistachios—and especially pistachio ice cream—were a favorite of Jean's dad. Being the quintessential daddy's girl, she created this super-nutty cake—with a chocolate twist—as a tribute to him. Bonus points if you serve this on Father's Day. (You'll have extra wafers left over after assembling your cake—lucky you! Store them in a resealable plastic bag in the freezer and enjoy them for up to 1 month.)

One 9-by-5-by-3-in/23-by-12-by-7.5-cm loaf pan

One 10-in/25-cm oval or rectangular serving platter

PISTACHIO WAFERS

MAKES ABOUT SIXTY 2¼-IN/5.5-CM WAFERS

2¼ cups/305 g all-purpose flour

½ tsp salt

1 cup/200 g granulated sugar

¾ cup/170 g unsalted butter, at room temperature

1½ tsp pure vanilla extract

1 tsp almond extract, or to taste

2 Tbsp whole milk

1 Tbsp light corn syrup

1 cup/240 g Pistachio Paste (page 35)

PISTACHIO-CHOCOLATE WHIPPED CREAM

MAKES ABOUT 6 CUPS/840 G

3 cups/720 ml heavy cream

½ cup/120 g Pistachio Paste (page 35)

⅓ cup/45 g confectioners' sugar

⅓ cup/35 g Dutch-process cocoa powder

¼ tsp almond extract, or to taste

⅛ tsp salt

Coarsely chopped toasted pistachios (see box, page 35) for decorating

→

In a medium bowl, whisk together the flour and salt.

In the bowl of a stand mixer fitted with the paddle attachment, cream the granulated sugar, butter, vanilla, and almond extract on medium-low speed until slightly fluffy, about 2 minutes. Be careful not to overbeat. Scrape the sides of the bowl with a rubber spatula.

In a small bowl, whisk the milk and corn syrup to combine. Add the milk mixture to the butter-sugar mixture with the mixer on medium-low speed; beat until just combined. Scrape the sides of the bowl with the rubber spatula. Add the pistachio paste and beat just until incorporated.

Add the flour mixture all at once to the mixer bowl. With the mixer on low speed, beat until the dough just begins to pull away from the bottom of the bowl and forms a cohesive mass. Scrape the sides of the bowl to fully incorporate all the ingredients.

Divide the dough in half and place each half on a sheet of plastic wrap. Loosely wrap the dough and form each half into a log about 2 in/5 cm wide. Roll the logs along the counter, still wrapped in plastic wrap, in order to shape into perfect cylinders. Tighten the plastic wrap around the logs and freeze them for at least 2 hours, or overnight. If you have trouble forming the soft dough into logs, form the dough into a disk (or loose log shape), wrap it in plastic wrap, and place in the freezer for about 20 minutes, just until it is cold enough to shape into the necessary log. Line two baking sheets with parchment paper.

Once frozen, unwrap one of the logs and use a sharp paring or chef's knife to cut it into thin slices about ⅛ in/3 mm thick; rotate the log as you slice, or the side sitting on the cutting surface will flatten. Arrange the slices about 1 in/2.5 cm apart on one of the prepared baking sheets and place in the freezer for at least 10 minutes. Repeat with the second dough log and prepared baking sheet. If you need more room to fit all your dough slices, simply arrange them on additional sheets of parchment paper, layer the dough-covered papers one on top of the other on the second baking sheet in the freezer, and switch them out as you bake off each batch. (You can also wrap the baking sheets in plastic wrap and freeze the rounds for up to 1 week.)

Position a rack in the center of the oven and preheat to 350°F/180°C.

Place one baking sheet of the frozen dough rounds in the oven and bake until they begin to brown just around the edges, 10 to 12 minutes, rotating the sheet halfway through the baking time. Using a stiff metal or plastic spatula, immediately press down lightly on each cookie to flatten it. Let the wafers cool on the baking sheet for 2 to 3 minutes, then transfer them to a wire rack to cool completely. The wafers should be very crispy when cooled. If they are not, place them back in the 350°F/180°C oven for 1 to 2 minutes more. Repeat to bake the additional sheets of frozen dough rounds.

TOASTING PISTACHIOS

Place shelled pistachios on a baking sheet in a 350°F/180°C oven until they begin to brown and become fragrant, 10 to 15 minutes. Stir the nuts a bit with a spatula midway through baking to ensure even toasting.

PISTACHIO PASTE

In a food processor, combine 2 cups/240 g shelled unsalted pistachios and ½ cups/100 g granulated sugar and pulse until the nuts are finely chopped, about 90 seconds. Do not overprocess, or the nuts will get too buttery.

Transfer the processed pistachios to the bowl of a stand mixer fitted with the paddle attachment. Add ¼ cup/60 ml water and 2 Tbsp room-temperature butter and beat on medium speed just until a thick paste forms. The paste will keep tightly covered in the refrigerator for up to 2 weeks.

MAKES ABOUT 1½ CUPS/360 G

Store the wafers in an airtight container as soon as they have cooled. They will remain crispy at room temperature, tightly sealed, for about 24 hours. Freezing the baked wafers in a resealable plastic bag also works well, for up to 1 month. There is no need to defrost the wafers before assembling your cake.

MAKE ❧ WHIPPED CREAM

Refrigerate the bowl of a stand mixer and the whisk attachment (or a medium metal bowl and beaters from a hand mixer) until quite cold, about 15 minutes.

Once chilled, remove the bowl and whisk from the refrigerator, add the cream, and whip it on medium speed until just thickened.

Add the pistachio paste, confectioners' sugar, cocoa powder, almond extract, and salt and, on medium-high speed, whip the cream until it holds stiff peaks that stand upright when the whisk is raised (the stiffer the cream, the more support it will provide the wafers in your cake). Use it immediately.

→

Line the loaf pan with plastic wrap that hangs slightly over the pan sides. Using a small offset spatula or the back of a spoon, spread a generous layer of the whipped cream on the bottom of the lined pan.

Cover as much of the cream as possible with a layer of the wafers, filling any gaps with broken wafers. The pieces should touch. The goal is a solid layer of wafers.

Continue layering whipped cream and wafers until you run out or reach the top of the pan, ending with the whipped cream. Gently cover the cake with plastic wrap. Refrigerate for 24 hours.

Peel the plastic wrap from the cake, place the serving platter over the cake, and invert the cake onto the platter. Carefully remove the pan and plastic-wrap lining and sprinkle the cake with coarsely chopped toasted pistachios. Using a knife, cut it into slices and serve.

BLACKBERRY-CHOCOLATE

YIELD: 9 TO 12 SERVINGS

The blackberries in this cake provide an excuse—not that we need one—for making a chocolate dessert even in the heat of summer. Crème de mûres blackberry liqueur adds sophistication to this dish. (You'll have extra graham crackers left over after assembling your cake—lucky you! Store them in a resealable plastic bag in the freezer and enjoy them for up to 1 month.)

One 8-by-8-by-2-in/20-by-20-by-5-cm square baking pan

GRAHAM CRACKERS

MAKES ABOUT THIRTY-SIX
2½-BY-5-IN/6-BY-12-CM CRACKERS

2¼ cups/305 g all-purpose flour

1½ cups/210 g whole-wheat flour

1½ tsp baking soda

Rounded 1 tsp salt

5 Tbsp/70 ml whole milk

1½ Tbsp pure vanilla extract

Rounded 1 cup/230 g packed dark brown sugar

5 Tbsp/70 g unsalted butter, at room temperature

¼ cup/60 ml vegetable oil

⅓ cup/105 g honey

MACERATED BLACKBERRIES

MAKES ABOUT 1¼ CUPS/535 G

4 cups/455 g fresh blackberries

3 to 4 Tbsp granulated sugar

1½ Tbsp freshly squeezed lemon juice (see box, page 45)

→

CHOCOLATE-BLACKBERRY PUDDING

MAKES ABOUT 5 CUPS/1 KG

1 cup/200 g granulated sugar

½ cup/50 g Dutch-process cocoa powder

¼ cup/35 g cornstarch

¾ tsp salt

2½ cups/600 ml whole milk

¾ cup/175 ml heavy cream

1 egg, lightly beaten

¼ cup/60 ml blackberry liqueur (crème de mûres), or to taste

1 Tbsp unsalted butter, at room temperature

2 tsp pure vanilla extract

BLACKBERRY WHIPPED CREAM

MAKES ABOUT 3 CUPS/420 G

1½ cups/360 ml heavy cream

¼ cup/60 ml blackberry liqueur (crème de mûres)

3 Tbsp confectioners' sugar

½ tsp pure vanilla extract

Fresh blackberries for decorating

MAKE *the* GRAHAM CRACKERS

In a medium bowl, whisk together both flours, the baking soda, and salt and set aside. In a small bowl, combine the milk and vanilla and set aside.

In the bowl of a stand mixer fitted with the paddle attachment, cream the brown sugar, butter, and vegetable oil on medium-low speed until slightly fluffy, about 2 minutes. Be careful not to overbeat. Scrape the sides of the bowl with a rubber spatula. Add the honey and mix until just incorporated and scrape the bowl again. The mixture may look a bit curdled at this point; that's okay.

With the mixer running on medium-low speed, add half of the flour mixture. Stop the machine and scrape the sides of the bowl. Return to medium-low speed and add the milk mixture, then the remaining flour mixture. Beat until the dough is still crumbly, and not yet a cohesive mass. Scrape the sides of the bowl to fully incorporate all the ingredients.

Form the dough into two 2½-by-5-in/ 6-by-12-cm blocks (or line an 8-by-4-in/ 20-by-10-cm loaf pan, preferably with straight sides, with plastic wrap and press the dough

→

into the pan, forming one large block), wrap the blocks (or pan) in plastic wrap, and freeze them for at least 2 hours, or overnight. (If you choose to press your dough into a loaf pan to shape it, your crackers will be slightly smaller than the traditional cracker size.)

Line two baking sheets with parchment paper.

Once frozen, unwrap one block of dough and use a sharp paring or chef's knife to cut it into thin rectangular slices about ⅛ in/3 mm thick. Do not be concerned if your rectangles are imperfect. (The crackers will be buried inside the cake and no one will know.) Using the tines of a fork, prick the rectangles lengthwise in two rows.

Arrange the slices about 1 in/2.5 cm apart on one of the prepared baking sheets and place them in the freezer for at least 10 minutes. Repeat with the second block of dough and prepared baking sheet. If you need more room to fit all of your dough slices, simply arrange them on additional sheets of parchment paper, layer the dough-covered papers one on top of the other on the second baking sheet in the freezer, and switch them out as you bake off each batch. (You can also wrap the baking sheets in plastic wrap and freeze the slices for up to 1 week.)

Position a rack in the center of the oven and preheat to 350°F/180°C.

Place one baking sheet of frozen dough slices in the oven and bake until they are golden brown and relatively firm and dry, 13 to 15 minutes, rotating the sheet halfway through the baking time. Using a stiff metal or plastic spatula, immediately press down lightly on each cracker to flatten it. Let the crackers cool on the baking sheet for 2 to 3 minutes, then transfer them to a wire rack to cool completely. The crackers should be very crispy when cooled. If they are not, place them back in the 350°F/180°C oven for 1 to 2 minutes more. Repeat to bake the additional sheets of frozen dough slices.

Store the crackers in an airtight container as soon as they have cooled. They will remain crispy at room temperature, tightly sealed, for about 24 hours. Freezing the baked crackers in a resealable plastic bag also works well, for up to 1 month. There is no need to defrost the crackers before assembling your cake.

MAKE the MACERATED BLACKBERRIES

In a medium bowl, combine the berries, 3 Tbsp of the granulated sugar, and the lemon juice and mash lightly with a rubber spatula, breaking up the larger berries. Add more sugar if needed, depending on the sweetness of the berries. Let the berries sit for at least 20 minutes before using. They are best used the day they are made.

MAKE the PUDDING

In a medium saucepan, combine the granulated sugar, cocoa powder, cornstarch, and salt. Add the milk and cream and whisk to combine. Add the egg, whisk again, and place the saucepan over medium-high heat, whisking constantly.

Once the mixture begins to thicken and bubbles begin popping on the surface, turn the heat to medium and whisk vigorously for 45 seconds. Remove the pan from the heat.

If the pudding has any lumps, strain it through a medium-mesh wire sieve into a heatproof bowl. Add the blackberry liqueur, butter, and vanilla and whisk until they are incorporated.

The pudding should be used almost immediately; it should still be warm and relatively pourable when you layer it with the crackers.

MAKE *the* WHIPPED CREAM

Refrigerate the bowl of a stand mixer and the whisk attachment (or a medium metal bowl and beaters from a hand mixer) until quite cold, about 15 minutes.

Once chilled, remove the bowl and whisk from the refrigerator, add the cream, and whip it on medium speed until just thickened.

Add the blackberry liqueur, confectioners' sugar, and vanilla and, on medium-high speed, whip the cream until it holds stiff peaks that stand upright when the whisk is raised. Use it immediately.

Using a small offset spatula or the back of a spoon, spread a generous layer of the pudding on the bottom of the baking pan.

Cover as much of the pudding as possible with a layer of the graham crackers, filling any gaps with broken crackers. The pieces should touch. The goal is a solid layer of graham crackers.

Spread a layer of the macerated blackberries over the crackers.

Continue layering in this order (pudding, crackers, blackberries) until you run out or reach the top of the pan. Spread the top of the cake with the whipped cream and gently cover it with plastic wrap. Refrigerate for 24 hours.

Peel the plastic wrap from the cake and top the cake with the fresh blackberries. Serve portions directly from the pan.

CHOCOLATE– GRAND MARNIER

YIELD: 9 TO 12 SERVINGS

This cake is all about the simple, yet ideal, marriage of chocolate and orange. Grand Marnier infuses the rich chocolate pudding and whipped cream, but orange juice and zest also make their way into the cream, ensuring the perfect ratio of orange to chocolate in every bite.

One 8-by-8-by-2-in/20-by-20-by-5-cm square baking pan

CHOCOLATE– GRAND MARNIER PUDDING

MAKES ABOUT 5 CUPS/1 KG

1 cup/200 g granulated sugar

½ cup/50 g Dutch-process cocoa powder

¼ cup/35 g cornstarch

¾ tsp salt

2½ cups/600 ml whole milk

¾ cup/180 ml heavy cream

1 egg, lightly beaten

¼ cup/60 ml Grand Marnier, or to taste

1 Tbsp unsalted butter, at room temperature

2 tsp orange extract

GRAND MARNIER WHIPPED CREAM

MAKES ABOUT 3 CUPS/420 G

1½ cups/360 ml heavy cream

¼ cup/60 ml Grand Marnier

3 Tbsp confectioners' sugar

1 Tbsp finely grated orange zest (see box, page 45)

1 Tbsp freshly squeezed orange juice (see box, page 45)

1 tsp orange extract, or to taste

ONE RECIPE LADYFINGERS

(PAGE 54)

Thinly sliced peeled and seeded oranges for decorating

→

MAKE *the* PUDDING

In a medium saucepan, combine the granulated sugar, cocoa powder, cornstarch, and salt. Add the milk and cream and whisk to combine. Add the egg, whisk again, and place the saucepan over medium-high heat, whisking constantly.

Once the mixture begins to thicken and bubbles begin popping on the surface, turn the heat to medium and whisk vigorously for 45 seconds. Remove the pan from the heat.

If the pudding has any lumps, strain it through a medium-mesh wire sieve into a heatproof bowl. Add the Grand Marnier, butter, and orange extract and whisk until they are incorporated.

The pudding should be used almost immediately; it should still be warm and relatively pourable when you layer it with the ladyfingers.

MAKE *the* WHIPPED CREAM

Refrigerate the bowl of a stand mixer and the whisk attachment (or a medium metal bowl and beaters from a hand mixer) until quite cold, about 15 minutes.

Once chilled, remove the bowl and whisk from the refrigerator, add the cream, and whip it on medium speed until just thickened.

Add the Grand Marnier, confectioners' sugar, orange zest, orange juice, and orange extract and, on medium-high speed, whip the cream until it holds stiff peaks that stand upright when the whisk is raised. Use it immediately.

Using a small offset spatula or the back of a spoon, spread a generous layer of the pudding on the bottom of the baking pan.

Cover as much of the pudding as possible with a layer of the ladyfingers, filling any gaps with broken ladyfingers. The pieces should touch. The goal is a solid layer of ladyfingers.

Continue layering pudding and ladyfingers until you run out or reach the top of the pan. Spread the top of the cake with the whipped cream and gently cover it with plastic wrap. Refrigerate for 24 hours.

Peel the plastic wrap from the cake and top the cake with orange slices in a decorative pattern. Serve portions directly from the pan.

ZESTING AND JUICING CITRUS

The amount of zest and juice you will get from your oranges, lemons, and limes will depend on the size and freshness of your produce. We use large, fresh fruit for our zesting and juicing purposes and usually get about 2 Tbsp zest and ⅓ cup/75 ml juice per orange; 1 Tbsp zest and 2 to 3 Tbsp juice per lemon; 1½ tsp zest and 1 to 2 Tbsp juice per Persian lime; and 1 tsp zest and 1 Tbsp juice per Key lime.

WHITE CHOCOLATE–ORANGE

YIELD: 9 TO 12 SERVINGS

White chocolate pudding is the perfect addition to an icebox cake, particularly when the sweetness of the pudding is counterbalanced with the tartness of the orange whipped cream.

One 8-by-8-by-2-in/20-by-20-by-5-cm square baking pan

WHITE CHOCOLATE PUDDING

MAKES ABOUT 5 CUPS/1 KG

2 Tbsp granulated sugar

¼ cup/35 g cornstarch

¾ tsp salt

2½ cups/600 ml whole milk

¾ cup/180 ml heavy cream

1 egg, lightly beaten

1¼ cups/200 g white chocolate chips, melted (see box, page 49) and cooled slightly

1 Tbsp unsalted butter, at room temperature

2 tsp pure vanilla extract

ORANGE WHIPPED CREAM

MAKES ABOUT 3 CUPS/360 G

1½ cups/360 ml heavy cream

¼ cup/35 g confectioners' sugar

1½ Tbsp finely grated orange zest (see box, page 45)

3 Tbsp freshly squeezed orange juice (see box, page 45)

2 tsp orange extract, or to taste

ONE RECIPE GRAHAM CRACKERS

(PAGE 37)

Orange sanding sugar for decorating (optional)

→

MAKE *the* PUDDING

In a medium saucepan, combine the granulated sugar, cornstarch, and salt. Add the milk and cream and whisk to combine. Add the egg, whisk again, and place the saucepan over medium-high heat, whisking constantly.

Once the mixture begins to thicken and bubbles begin popping on the surface, turn the heat to medium and whisk vigorously for 45 seconds. Remove the pan from the heat.

If the pudding has any lumps, strain it through a medium-mesh wire sieve into a heatproof bowl. Add the white chocolate, butter, and vanilla and whisk until they are incorporated.

The pudding should be used almost immediately; it should still be warm and relatively pourable when you layer it with the crackers.

MAKE *the* WHIPPED CREAM

Refrigerate the bowl of a stand mixer and the whisk attachment (or a medium metal bowl and beaters from a hand mixer) until quite cold, about 15 minutes.

Once chilled, remove the bowl and whisk from the refrigerator, add the cream, and whip it on medium speed until just thickened.

Add the confectioners' sugar, orange zest, orange juice, and orange extract and, on medium-high speed, whip the cream until it holds stiff peaks that stand upright when the whisk is raised. Use it immediately.

Using a small offset spatula or the back of a spoon, spread a generous layer of the pudding on the bottom of the baking pan.

Cover as much of the pudding as possible with a layer of the graham crackers, filling any gaps with broken crackers. The pieces should touch. The goal is a solid layer of graham crackers.

Continue layering pudding and crackers until you run out or reach the top of the pan. Spread the top of the cake with the whipped cream and gently cover it with plastic wrap. Refrigerate for 24 hours.

Peel the plastic wrap from the cake and sprinkle orange sanding sugar (if using) over the top of the cake. Serve portions directly from the pan.

MELTING CHOCOLATE

Place the chocolate in a small microwave-safe bowl and microwave it on high in 15-second increments, stirring after each increment, until melted. Alternatively, create a double boiler by placing the chocolate in a small heatproof bowl nested over (but not touching) a small pot of simmering water over medium-low heat. Stir gently until melted.

RED VELVET

YIELD: 12 TO 15 SERVINGS

Red velvet cake is always a winner at birthday parties and other celebrations. Our icebox version is extra chocolatey and includes a surprising cinnamon–cream cheese whipped cream. (You'll have extra wafers left over after assembling your cake—lucky you! Store them in a resealable plastic bag in the freezer and enjoy them for up to 1 month.)

One 9-by-5-by-3-in/23-by-12-by-7.5-cm loaf pan

One 10-in/25-cm oval or rectangular serving platter

RED VELVET WAFERS

MAKES ABOUT SIXTY
2¼-IN/5.5-CM WAFERS

2 cups minus 2 Tbsp/250 g all-purpose flour

2 Tbsp Dutch-process cocoa powder

½ tsp salt

1¼ cups/250 g granulated sugar

¾ cup/170 g unsalted butter, at room temperature

2 tsp pure vanilla extract

2 Tbsp whole milk

1 Tbsp light corn syrup

1 Tbsp red food coloring

CINNAMON–CREAM CHEESE WHIPPED CREAM

MAKES ABOUT 7 CUPS/1.1 KG

1½ cups/340 g cream cheese, at room temperature

3 cups/720 ml heavy cream

1 cup/130 g confectioners' sugar

1 Tbsp pure vanilla extract

1½ tsp ground cinnamon

Ground cinnamon for decorating

→

MAKE *the* WAFERS

In a medium bowl, whisk together the flour, cocoa powder, and salt.

In the bowl of a stand mixer fitted with the paddle attachment, cream the granulated sugar, butter, and vanilla on medium-low speed until slightly fluffy, about 2 minutes. Be careful not to overbeat. Scrape the sides of the bowl with a rubber spatula.

In a small bowl, whisk the milk, corn syrup, and food coloring to combine. Add the milk mixture to the butter-sugar mixture with the mixer on medium-low speed; beat until just combined. Scrape the sides of the bowl with the rubber spatula.

Add the flour mixture all at once to the mixer bowl. With the mixer on low speed, beat until the dough just begins to pull away from the bottom of the bowl and forms a cohesive mass. Scrape the sides of the bowl to fully incorporate all the ingredients.

Divide the dough in half and place each half on a sheet of plastic wrap. Loosely wrap the dough and form each half into a log about 2 in/5 cm wide. Roll the logs along the counter, still wrapped in plastic wrap, in order to shape into perfect cylinders. Tighten the plastic wrap around the logs and freeze them for at least 2 hours, or overnight. If you have trouble forming the soft dough into logs, form the dough into a disk (or loose log shape), wrap it in plastic wrap, and place in the freezer for about

20 minutes, just until it is cold enough to shape into the necessary log. Line two baking sheets with parchment paper.

Once frozen, unwrap one of the logs and use a sharp paring or chef's knife to cut it into thin slices about ⅛ in/3 mm thick; rotate the log as you slice, or the side sitting on the cutting surface will flatten. Arrange the slices about 1 in/2.5 cm apart on one of the prepared baking sheets and place in the freezer for at least 10 minutes. Repeat with the second dough log and prepared baking sheet. If you need more room to fit all your dough slices, simply arrange them on additional sheets of parchment paper, layer the dough-covered papers one on top of the other on the second baking sheet in the freezer, and switch them out as you bake off each batch. (You can also wrap the baking sheets in plastic wrap and freeze the rounds for up to 1 week.)

Position a rack in the center of the oven and preheat to 350°F/180°C.

Place one baking sheet of the frozen dough rounds in the oven and bake until they appear dry, 10 to 12 minutes, rotating the sheet halfway through the baking time. Using a stiff metal or plastic spatula, immediately press down lightly on each cookie to flatten it. Let the wafers cool on the baking sheet for 2 to 3 minutes, then transfer them to a wire rack to cool completely. The wafers should be very crispy when cooled. If they are not, place them back in the 350°F/180°C oven for 1 to 2 minutes more. Repeat to bake the additional sheets of dough rounds.

Store the wafers in an airtight container as soon as they have cooled. They will remain crispy at room temperature, tightly sealed, for about 24 hours. Freezing the baked wafers in a resealable plastic bag also works well, for up to 1 month. There is no need to defrost the wafers before assembling your cake.

MAKE *the* WHIPPED CREAM

Refrigerate the bowl of a stand mixer and the whisk attachment (or a medium metal bowl and beaters from a hand mixer) until quite cold, about 15 minutes.

Once chilled, remove the bowl and whisk from the refrigerator, add the cream cheese, and whip it on medium speed until smooth. Add the cream and continue to whip on medium speed until the cream is incorporated.

Add the confectioners' sugar, vanilla, and cinnamon and, on medium-high speed, whip the cream mixture until it holds stiff peaks that stand upright when the whisk is raised (the stiffer the cream, the more support it will provide the wafers in your cake). Use it immediately.

Line the loaf pan with plastic wrap that hangs slightly over the pan sides. Using a small offset spatula or the back of a spoon, spread a generous layer of the whipped cream on the bottom of the lined pan.

Cover as much of the cream as possible with a layer of the wafers, filling any gaps with broken wafers. The pieces should touch. The goal is a solid layer of wafers.

Continue layering whipped cream and wafers until you run out or reach the top of the pan, ending with whipped cream. Gently cover the cake with plastic wrap. Refrigerate for 24 hours.

Peel the plastic wrap from the cake, place the serving platter over the cake, and invert the cake onto the platter. Carefully remove the pan and plastic-wrap lining and lightly dust the cake with ground cinnamon. Using a knife, cut it into slices and serve.

BLACK FOREST

YIELD: 9 TO 12 SERVINGS

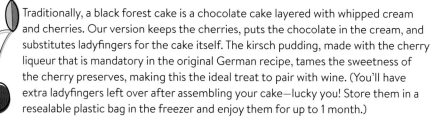 Traditionally, a black forest cake is a chocolate cake layered with whipped cream and cherries. Our version keeps the cherries, puts the chocolate in the cream, and substitutes ladyfingers for the cake itself. The kirsch pudding, made with the cherry liqueur that is mandatory in the original German recipe, tames the sweetness of the cherry preserves, making this the ideal treat to pair with wine. (You'll have extra ladyfingers left over after assembling your cake—lucky you! Store them in a resealable plastic bag in the freezer and enjoy them for up to 1 month.)

One 8-by-8-by-2-in/20-by-20-by-5-cm
square baking pan

LADYFINGERS

MAKES ABOUT SIXTY-SIX
3-BY-1-IN/7.5-BY-2.5-CM
LADYFINGERS

6 eggs, separated

½ cup/100 g granulated sugar,
plus 3 Tbsp

1½ tsp pure vanilla extract

1 cup/135 g all-purpose flour

½ tsp salt

Confectioners' sugar for dusting

KIRSCH PUDDING

MAKES ABOUT 5 CUPS/1 KG

1 cup/200 g granulated sugar

¼ cup/35 g cornstarch

¾ tsp salt

2½ cups/600 ml whole milk

¾ cup/180 ml heavy cream

1 egg, lightly beaten

¼ cup/60 ml kirsch, or to taste

1 Tbsp unsalted butter, at room
temperature

2 tsp pure vanilla extract

→

CHOCOLATE-KIRSCH WHIPPED CREAM

MAKES ABOUT 3 CUPS/420 G

1½ cups/360 ml heavy cream

¼ cup/35 g confectioners' sugar

¼ cup/60 ml kirsch, or to taste

½ tsp pure vanilla extract

3 Tbsp Dutch-process
cocoa powder, sifted

A generous 2 cups/740 g cherry
preserves, whisked vigorously to ease
spreadability, if necessary

Cocoa powder (optional) and fresh
cherries for decorating

MAKE *the* LADYFINGERS

Position a rack in the center of the oven and preheat to 350°F/180°C. Line two baking sheets with parchment paper.

In the bowl of a stand mixer fitted with the whisk attachment, beat the egg yolks, ½ cup/100 g granulated sugar, and vanilla on medium-high speed until the mixture doubles in volume, is very yellow, and falls in a ribbon when the whisk is lifted out of the bowl, about 5 minutes (7 to 9 minutes if using a hand mixer).

Sift the flour over the mixer bowl and very gently fold it into the yolk mixture with a rubber spatula. The batter will be very thick. Transfer the batter to a large bowl and clean the mixer bowl and whisk attachment.

In the clean mixer bowl, fitted again with the whisk attachment, whisk the egg whites and salt on medium speed until soft peaks form (the peaks should flop over when the whisk is lifted from the bowl). Add the remaining 3 Tbsp granulated sugar, 1 Tbsp at a time, whisking to incorporate after each addition, and then whisk for 5 minutes, until stiff peaks form (the peaks should stand upright when the whisk is lifted from the bowl).

In three batches, gently fold the beaten whites into the yolk mixture until just incorporated, being very careful not to decrease the volume you've just created. Your batter might look a bit curdled; that's okay.

Fit a large pastry bag with a ½-in/12-mm #806 Ateco round tip, or use a large, heavy-duty resealable plastic bag and snip off a small to medium hole from the corner. Fill the bag with batter and pipe 3-by-1-in/7.5-by-2.5-cm fingers onto each of the prepared baking sheets, five to seven ladyfingers per row, and up to twenty-five ladyfingers per sheet (they don't spread very much). Unless you have several baking sheets, you will need to reuse your sheets to finish piping the batter.

Just before baking each sheet, generously dust confectioners' sugar over the ladyfingers, leaving a thick coat of sugar, which will create a nice, crunchy crust when baked.

Place one baking sheet of ladyfingers in the oven and bake until they are puffy, dry to the touch, and just very slightly browned, 10 to 12 minutes, rotating the sheet halfway through the baking time. Let the ladyfingers cool on the baking sheet for 1 to 2 minutes. When they are still warm, use a small offset or other thin spatula to transfer them to a wire rack to cool completely. Repeat with any leftover batter on cooled baking sheets.

Store the ladyfingers tightly covered at room temperature for up to 3 days. Freezing the ladyfingers in a resealable plastic bag also works well, for up to 1 month. There is no need to defrost the ladyfingers before assembling your cake.

MAKE *the* PUDDING

In a medium saucepan, combine the granulated sugar, cornstarch, and salt. Add the milk and cream and whisk to combine. Add the egg, whisk again, and place the saucepan over medium-high heat, whisking constantly.

Once the mixture begins to thicken and bubbles begin popping on the surface, turn the heat to medium and whisk vigorously for 45 seconds. Remove the pan from the heat.

If the pudding has any lumps, strain it through a medium-mesh wire sieve into a heatproof bowl. Add the kirsch, butter, and vanilla and whisk until they are incorporated.

The pudding should be used almost immediately; it should still be warm and relatively pourable when you layer it with the ladyfingers.

MAKE *the* WHIPPED CREAM

Refrigerate the bowl of a stand mixer and the whisk attachment (or a medium metal bowl and beaters from a hand mixer) until quite cold, about 15 minutes.

Once chilled, remove the bowl and whisk from the refrigerator, add the cream, and whip it on medium speed until just thickened.

Add the confectioners' sugar, kirsch, vanilla, and cocoa powder and, on medium-high speed, whip the cream until it holds stiff peaks that stand upright when the whisk is raised. Use it immediately.

→

57

_____

Using a small offset spatula or the back of a spoon, spread a generous layer of the pudding on the bottom of the baking pan.

Cover as much of the pudding as possible with a layer of the ladyfingers, filling any gaps with broken ladyfingers. The pieces should touch. The goal is a solid layer of ladyfingers.

Generously spread a layer of the preserves over the ladyfingers.

Continue layering in this order (pudding, ladyfingers, preserves) until you run out or reach the top of the pan. Spread the top of the cake with the whipped cream and gently cover it with plastic wrap. Refrigerate for 24 hours.

Peel the plastic wrap from the cake and lightly dust the cake with cocoa powder, if desired, and top with the fresh cherries. Serve portions directly from the pan.

ESPRESSO CHIP

Our espresso chip icebox cake is reminiscent of tiramisu; however, we've added the delightful texture of mini chocolate chips, amped up the espresso flavor, and made it even creamier. This cake is ideally consumed after large plates of spaghetti and meatballs.

One 9-by-3-in/23-by-7.5-cm springform pan

ESPRESSO PUDDING

MAKES ABOUT 6 CUPS/1.3 KG

1⅓ cups/265 g granulated sugar

6 Tbsp/50 g cornstarch

¼ cup/15 g espresso powder

1 tsp salt

3½ cups/840 ml whole milk

1 cup/240 ml heavy cream

2 eggs, lightly beaten

2 Tbsp unsalted butter, at room temperature

1 Tbsp pure vanilla extract

13 oz/370 g mini semisweet chocolate chips

ESPRESSO-MASCARPONE WHIPPED CREAM

MAKES ABOUT 7 CUPS/775 G

3 Tbsp espresso powder

3 Tbsp boiling water

1½ cups/360 ml heavy cream

1½ cups/340 g mascarpone cheese, at room temperature

½ cup/65 g confectioners' sugar

⅓ cup/75 ml Kahlúa

Pinch of salt

ONE RECIPE LADYFINGERS

(PAGE 54)

Crushed chocolate-covered espresso beans or mini semisweet chocolate chips for decorating

MAKE *the* PUDDING

In a large saucepan, combine the granulated sugar, cornstarch, espresso powder, and salt. Add the milk and cream and whisk to combine. Add the eggs, whisk again, and place the saucepan over medium-high heat, whisking constantly.

Once the mixture begins to thicken and bubbles begin popping on the surface, turn the heat to medium and whisk vigorously for 45 seconds. Remove the pan from the heat.

If the pudding has any lumps, strain it through a medium-mesh wire sieve into a heatproof bowl. Add the butter and vanilla and whisk until they are incorporated.

The pudding should be used almost immediately; it should still be warm and relatively pourable when you layer it with the ladyfingers.

MAKE *the* WHIPPED CREAM

Refrigerate the bowl of a stand mixer and the whisk attachment (or a medium metal bowl and beaters from a hand mixer) until quite cold, about 15 minutes.

In a small bowl, combine the espresso powder with the boiling water and set them aside to cool.

Once chilled, remove the mixer bowl and whisk from the refrigerator, add the cream and mascarpone, and whip them on medium speed until combined.

Add the cooled espresso mixture, confectioners' sugar, Kahlúa, and salt and, on medium-high speed, whip the cream until it holds stiff peaks that stand upright when the whisk is raised. Use it immediately.

Lightly coat the sides of your springform pan with cooking spray, and line the sides of the pan with a 3-by-29-in/7.5-by-75-cm strip of parchment paper. Using a small offset spatula or the back of a spoon, spread a generous layer of the pudding on the bottom of the pan.

Generously sprinkle a layer of the mini chocolate chips over the pudding.

Cover as much of the pudding and chips as possible with a layer of the ladyfingers, filling any gaps with broken ladyfingers. The pieces should touch. The goal is a solid layer of ladyfingers.

Continue layering in this order (pudding, chips, ladyfingers) until you run out or reach the top of the pan, ending with pudding. Spread the whipped cream on top of the cake. Gently cover the cake with plastic wrap. Refrigerate for 24 hours.

Peel the plastic wrap from the cake and run a paring knife between the paper and the pan. Open the clamp, remove the pan sides, and gently peel back the parchment paper. Transfer the cake, still on the pan bottom, to a serving platter. Decorate with crushed chocolate-covered espresso beans. Using a knife, slice into wedges and serve, dolloped with any leftover whipped cream.

BLACK-AND-WHITE MALTED

YIELD: 15 TO 20 SERVINGS

Jessie's love of Whoppers (and extra-thick malted milkshakes) inspired this cake. Malt alone gives vanilla a creamy, slightly nutty dimension, and is also the perfect foil to the sweetness of milk chocolate.

One 9-by-3-in/23-by-7.5-cm springform pan

VANILLA WAFERS

MAKES ABOUT SIXTY
2¼-IN/5.5-CM WAFERS

2 cups/270 g all-purpose flour

½ tsp salt

1¼ cups/250 g granulated sugar

¾ cup/170 g unsalted butter,
at room temperature

1 Tbsp pure vanilla extract

2 Tbsp whole milk

1 Tbsp light corn syrup

MILK CHOCOLATE GANACHE

MAKES A SCANT 2 CUPS/505 G

13 oz/370 g milk chocolate,
finely chopped

¼ tsp salt

¾ cup/180 ml heavy cream

MALT WHIPPED CREAM

MAKES ABOUT 8 CUPS/1.1 KG

1 qt/960 ml heavy cream

½ cup/170 g malted milk powder

½ cup/65 g confectioners' sugar

2 tsp pure vanilla extract

Crushed or chopped malted milk balls
for decorating

→

MAKE *the* WAFERS

In a medium bowl, whisk together the flour and salt.

In the bowl of a stand mixer fitted with the paddle attachment, cream the granulated sugar, butter, and vanilla on medium-low speed until slightly fluffy, about 2 minutes. Be careful not to overbeat. Scrape the sides of the bowl with a rubber spatula.

In a small bowl, whisk the milk and corn syrup to combine. Add the milk mixture to the butter-sugar mixture with the mixer on medium-low speed; beat until just combined. Scrape the sides of the bowl with the rubber spatula.

Add the flour mixture all at once to the mixer bowl. With the mixer on low speed, beat until the dough just begins to pull away from the bottom of the bowl and forms a cohesive mass. Scrape the sides of the bowl to fully incorporate all the ingredients.

Divide the dough in half and place each half on a sheet of plastic wrap. Loosely wrap the dough and form each half into a log about 2 in/5 cm wide. Roll the logs along the counter, still wrapped in plastic wrap, in order to shape into perfect cylinders. Tighten the plastic wrap around the logs and freeze them for at least 2 hours, or overnight. If you have trouble forming the soft dough into logs, form the dough into a disk (or loose log shape), wrap it in plastic wrap, and place in the freezer for about 20 minutes, just until it is cold enough to shape into the necessary log. Line two baking sheets with parchment paper.

Once frozen, unwrap one of the logs and use a sharp paring or chef's knife to cut it into thin slices about 1/8 in/3 mm thick; rotate the log as you slice, or the side sitting on the cutting surface will flatten. Arrange the slices about 1 in/2.5 cm apart on one of the prepared baking sheets and place in the freezer for at least 10 minutes. Repeat with the second dough log and prepared baking sheet. If you need more room to fit all your dough slices, simply arrange them on additional sheets of parchment paper, layer the dough-covered papers one on top of the other on the second baking sheet in the freezer, and switch them out as you bake off each batch. (You can also wrap the baking sheets in plastic wrap and freeze the rounds for up to 1 week.)

Position a rack in the center of the oven and preheat to 350°F/180°C.

Place one baking sheet of the frozen dough rounds in the oven and bake until they begin to brown just around the edges, 10 to 12 minutes, rotating the sheet halfway through the baking time. Using a stiff metal or plastic spatula, immediately press down lightly on each cookie to flatten it. Let the wafers cool on the baking sheet for 2 to 3 minutes, then transfer them to a wire rack to cool completely. The wafers should be very crispy when cooled. If they are not, place them back in the 350°F/180°C oven for 1 to 2 minutes more. Repeat to bake the additional sheets of frozen dough rounds.

Store the wafers in an airtight container as soon as they have cooled. They will remain crispy at room temperature, tightly sealed, for about 24 hours. Freezing the baked wafers in a resealable plastic bag also works well, for up to

1 month. There is no need to defrost the wafers before assembling your cake.

MAKE *the* GANACHE

Place the chocolate and salt in a medium heatproof bowl and set aside. In a small saucepan, heat the cream over medium-high heat just until bubbles begin to form around the edges.

Pour the warm cream over the chocolate and salt and let sit for 1 minute so it begins to melt. Gently whisk together until fully incorporated and shiny.

Let come to room temperature, stirring occasionally, until it thickens and is less like chocolate syrup and pours more like hot fudge.

(To make ahead, let cool to room temperature, cover, and refrigerate for up to 1 week. Reheat over medium-low heat until liquefied.)

MAKE *the* WHIPPED CREAM

Refrigerate the bowl of a stand mixer and the whisk attachment (or a medium metal bowl and beaters from a hand mixer) until quite cold, about 15 minutes.

Once chilled, remove the bowl and whisk from the refrigerator, add the cream, and whip it on medium speed until just thickened.

Add the malted milk powder, confectioners' sugar, and vanilla and, on medium-high speed, whip the cream until it holds stiff peaks that stand upright when the whisk is raised (the stiffer the cream, the more support it will provide the wafers in your cake). Use it immediately.

Lightly coat the sides of your springform pan with cooking spray and line the sides of the pan with a 3-by-29-in/7.5-by-75-cm strip of parchment paper. Using a small offset spatula or the back of a spoon, spread a generous layer of the whipped cream on the bottom of the pan.

Cover as much of the whipped cream as possible with a layer of the wafers, filling any gaps with broken wafers. The pieces should touch. The goal is a solid layer of wafers.

Generously spread a layer of the ganache over the wafers.

Continue layering in this order (whipped cream, wafers, ganache) until you run out or reach the top of the pan. Spread the top of the cake with a final layer of whipped cream and gently cover it with plastic wrap. Refrigerate for 24 hours.

Peel the plastic wrap from the cake and run a paring knife between the paper and the pan. Open the clamp, remove the pan sides, and gently peel back the parchment paper. Transfer the cake, still on the pan bottom, to a serving platter. Sprinkle crushed malted milk balls on top of the cake. Using a knife, slice into wedges and serve.

SALTY MILK DUD

Who doesn't love snacking on Milk Duds while watching a movie on the silver screen? It's a shame that sneaking a slice of this cake into a theater would be so darn messy. Our spin on the classic candy is sprinkled with flaky sea salt (we prefer Maldon), which makes for a slightly more adult treat. If you're sharing the cake with kids, you may want to omit the sea salt and just decorate with Milk Duds instead.

One 13-by-9-by-2-in/33-by-23-by-5-cm baking pan

CHOCOLATE GRAHAM CRACKERS

MAKES ABOUT THIRTY-SIX
2½-BY-5-IN/6-BY-12-CM CRACKERS

1¾ cups/235 g all-purpose flour

1 cup plus 2 Tbsp/160 g whole-wheat flour

¾ cup plus 2 Tbsp/90 g Dutch-process cocoa powder

1½ tsp baking soda

Rounded 1 tsp salt

5 Tbsp/70 ml whole milk

1½ Tbsp pure vanilla extract

Rounded 1 cup/230 g packed dark brown sugar

5 Tbsp/70 g unsalted butter, at room temperature

¼ cup/60 ml vegetable oil

⅓ cup/105 g honey

SALTY CARAMEL

MAKES ABOUT 1³/4 CUPS/455 G

2 cups/400 g granulated sugar

½ cup/120 ml water

1¼ cups/300 ml heavy cream, warmed

2 Tbsp unsalted butter

2 tsp pure vanilla extract

2 tsp kosher salt

→

SALTY CARAMEL
PUDDING

MAKES ABOUT 6 CUPS/1.3 KG

1 cup/240 ml heavy cream

6 Tbsp/50 g cornstarch

2 eggs, lightly beaten

1½ cups/300 g granulated sugar

2 Tbsp light corn syrup

⅔ cup/165 ml water

3½ cups/840 ml whole milk, warmed

3 Tbsp unsalted butter

1 Tbsp plus 1 tsp kosher salt

1 Tbsp pure vanilla extract

CHOCOLATE
WHIPPED CREAM

MAKES ABOUT 4 CUPS/480 G

2 cups/480 ml heavy cream

⅓ cup/45 g confectioners' sugar

¼ cup/25 g Dutch-process
cocoa powder, sifted

1 tsp pure vanilla extract

Flaky sea salt (such as Maldon) or
chopped Milk Duds or malted milk balls
for decorating

MAKE the CHOCOLATE
GRAHAM CRACKERS

In a medium bowl, whisk together both flours, the cocoa powder, baking soda, and salt and set aside. In a small bowl, combine the milk and vanilla and set aside.

In the bowl of a stand mixer fitted with the paddle attachment, cream the brown sugar, butter, and vegetable oil on medium-low speed until slightly fluffy, about 2 minutes. Be careful not to overbeat. Scrape the sides of the bowl with a rubber spatula. Add the honey and mix until just incorporated and scrape the bowl again. The mixture may look a bit curdled at this point; that's okay.

With the mixer running on medium-low speed, add half of the flour mixture. Stop the machine and scrape the sides of the bowl. Return to medium-low speed and add the milk mixture, then the remaining flour mixture. Beat until the dough is still crumbly, and not yet a cohesive mass. Scrape the sides of the bowl to fully incorporate all the ingredients.

Form the dough into two 2½-by-5-in/ 6-by-12-cm blocks (or line an 8-by-4-in/ 20-by-10-cm loaf pan, preferably with straight sides, with plastic wrap and press the dough into the pan, forming one large block), wrap the blocks (or pan) in plastic wrap, and freeze them for at least 2 hours, or overnight. (If you choose to press your dough into a loaf pan to shape it, your crackers will be slightly smaller than the traditional cracker size.)

Line two baking sheets with parchment paper.

Once frozen, unwrap one block of dough and use a sharp paring knife or chef's knife to cut it into thin rectangular slices about ⅛ in/ 3 mm thick. Do not be concerned if your rectangles are imperfect. (The crackers will be buried inside the cake and no one will know.) Using the tines of a fork, prick the rectangles lengthwise in two rows.

Arrange the slices about 1 in/2.5 cm apart on one of the prepared baking sheets and place in the freezer for at least 10 minutes. Repeat with the second block of dough and prepared baking sheet. If you need more room to fit all of your dough slices, simply arrange them on additional sheets of parchment paper, layer the dough-covered papers one on top of the other on the second baking sheet in the freezer, and switch them out as you bake off each batch. (You can also wrap the baking sheets in plastic wrap and freeze the slices for up to 1 week.)

Position a rack in the center of the oven and preheat to 350°F/180°C.

Place one baking sheet of the frozen dough slices in the oven and bake until they are relatively firm and dry, 13 to 15 minutes, rotating the sheet halfway through the baking time. Using a stiff metal or plastic spatula, immediately press down lightly on each cracker to flatten it. Let the crackers cool on the baking sheet for 2 to 3 minutes, then transfer them to a wire rack to cool completely. The crackers should be very crispy when cooled. If they are not, place them back in the 350°F/180°C oven for 1 to 2 minutes more. Repeat to bake the additional sheets of frozen dough slices.

Store the crackers in an airtight container as soon as they have cooled. They will remain crispy at room temperature, tightly sealed, for about 24 hours. Freezing the baked crackers in a resealable plastic bag also works well, for up to 1 month. There is no need to defrost the crackers before assembling your cake.

MAKE *the* CARAMEL

Put the granulated sugar and water in a small saucepan and whisk until combined. Place the saucepan over medium heat and cook, without stirring, until the sugar has dissolved. Increase the heat to medium-high and cook the sugar mixture until it colors to deep amber; occasionally hold the pan with pot holders and gently swirl the mixture to ensure that the sugar cooks evenly and that the color is to your liking (the deeper the color, the stronger the flavor of the caramel). Watch the mixture carefully as it cooks, since caramel goes quickly from brown to burnt. (If sugar crystals form on the sides of your pan, use a wet pastry brush to wipe them away.)

Remove the saucepan from the heat and pour in the warm cream—carefully, as the hot mixture may splatter. (Warming the cream first should prevent the caramel from hardening

→

69

and becoming clumpy [i.e., seizing], but if it does, return the saucepan to the heat and melt the hardened bits, stirring gently, until the caramel liquefies.) Add the butter, vanilla, and salt, stirring constantly with a wooden spoon or heatproof spatula until incorporated.

Transfer the caramel to a large heatproof liquid measuring cup (the easiest way to drizzle the caramel onto your cake layers) and let it cool to room temperature and slightly thickened. You can also place it in the refrigerator to speed up the cooling process.

The caramel will keep, tightly covered in the refrigerator, for up to 1 week. Bring to room temperature before using.

MAKE *the* PUDDING

In a medium bowl, whisk together the cream, cornstarch, and eggs and set aside.

Put the granulated sugar, corn syrup, and water in a medium saucepan and whisk until combined. Place the saucepan over medium heat and cook, without stirring, until the sugar has dissolved. Increase the heat to medium-high and cook the sugar mixture until it colors to deep amber; occasionally hold the pan with pot holders and gently swirl the mixture to ensure that the sugar cooks evenly and that the color is to your liking (the deeper the color, the stronger the flavor of the caramel). Watch the mixture carefully as it cooks, since caramel goes quickly from brown to burnt. (If sugar crystals form on the sides of your pan, use a wet pastry brush to wipe them away.)

Remove the saucepan from the heat and pour in the warm milk—carefully, as the mixture may splatter. (Warming the milk should prevent the caramel from hardening and becoming clumpy [i.e., seizing], but if it does, return the saucepan to the heat and melt the hardened bits, stirring gently, until the caramel liquefies.) Stir with a wooden spoon or heatproof spatula.

Slowly add the hot caramel-milk mixture to the egg mixture 2 to 3 Tbsp at a time to gently raise its temperature. Stir after each addition. Once the egg mixture has been warmed up a bit (i.e., tempered) by the hot caramel, pour it into the remaining caramel in the saucepan and place the pan over medium-high heat, whisking constantly.

Once the mixture begins to thicken and bubbles begin popping on the surface, turn the heat to medium and whisk vigorously for 45 seconds. Remove the pan from the heat.

If the pudding has any lumps, strain it through a medium-mesh wire sieve into a heatproof bowl. Add the butter, salt, and vanilla and whisk until they are incorporated.

The pudding should be used almost immed-iately; it should still be warm and relatively pourable when you layer it with the crackers.

MAKE ❖ WHIPPED CREAM

Refrigerate the bowl of a stand mixer and the whisk attachment (or a medium metal bowl and beaters from a hand mixer) until quite cold, about 15 minutes.

Once chilled, remove the bowl and whisk from the refrigerator; add the cream and whip it on medium speed until just thickened.

Add the confectioners' sugar, cocoa powder, and vanilla and, on medium-high speed, whip the cream until it holds stiff peaks that stand upright when the whisk is raised. Use it immediately.

Using a small offset spatula or the back of a spoon, spread a generous layer of the pudding on the bottom of the baking pan.

Cover as much of the pudding as possible with a layer of the graham crackers, filling any gaps with broken crackers. The pieces should touch. The goal is a solid layer of graham crackers.

Generously spread a layer of the caramel over the crackers.

Continue layering in this order (pudding, crackers, caramel) until you run out or reach the top of the pan. Spread the top of the cake with the whipped cream and gently cover it with plastic wrap. Refrigerate for 24 hours.

Peel the plastic wrap from the cake and lightly sprinkle flaky sea salt or chopped candy over the top of the cake. Serve portions directly from the pan.

S'MORE

YIELD: 15 TO 20 SERVINGS

The flavors of this iconic campfire dessert—no kindling required—can now be enjoyed year-round, thanks to this cake. There's no way you can miss with the combination of chocolate, marshmallow, and graham cracker. This cake is extra-special, with both pudding and whipped cream layered throughout.

One 9-by-3-in/23-by-7.5-cm springform pan

CHOCOLATE PUDDING

MAKES ABOUT 5 CUPS/1 KG

1 cup/200 g granulated sugar

½ cup/50 g Dutch-process cocoa powder

¼ cup/35 g cornstarch

¾ tsp salt

2½ cups/600 ml whole milk

¾ cup/180 ml heavy cream

1 egg, lightly beaten

1 Tbsp unsalted butter, at room temperature

2 tsp pure vanilla extract

MARSHMALLOW-CREAM WHIPPED CREAM

MAKES ABOUT 6 CUPS/795 G

3 egg whites, at room temperature

¾ tsp cream of tartar

¼ tsp salt

1 Tbsp granulated sugar, plus ¾ cup/150 g

¾ cup/180 ml light corn syrup

¼ cup/60 ml water

¾ tsp pure vanilla extract

2 cups/480 ml heavy cream

ONE RECIPE GRAHAM CRACKERS

(PAGE 37)

Crushed graham crackers or grated chocolate for decorating

→

MAKE *the* PUDDING

In a medium saucepan, combine the granulated sugar, cocoa powder, cornstarch, and salt. Add the milk and cream and whisk to combine. Add the egg, whisk again, and place the saucepan over medium-high heat, whisking constantly.

Once the mixture begins to thicken and bubbles begin popping on the surface, turn the heat to medium and whisk vigorously for 45 seconds. Remove the pan from the heat.

If the pudding has any lumps, strain it through a medium-mesh wire sieve into a heatproof bowl. Add the butter and vanilla and whisk until they are incorporated.

The pudding should be used almost immediately; it should still be warm and relatively pourable when you layer it with the crackers.

MAKE *the* WHIPPED CREAM

In the bowl of a stand mixer fitted with the whisk attachment, whisk together the egg whites, cream of tartar, and salt on medium speed until quite frothy. Add the 1 Tbsp granulated sugar and whisk until soft peaks form. The peaks should flop over when the whisk is lifted. Be careful not to overbeat.

Meanwhile, in a small saucepan over medium heat, combine the remaining ¾ cup/150 g granulated sugar, corn syrup, and water. Using a wooden spoon or heat-proof spatula, gently stir the mixture until the sugar dissolves completely. Attach a candy thermometer to the side of the pan. Increase the heat to medium-high and boil the mixture until it reaches the firm-ball stage, 246° to 248°F/ 118° to 120°C.

With the stand mixer on low, slowly add the sugar syrup to the beaten egg whites, aiming it away from the whisk. Increase the mixer speed to high and beat until the mixture reaches room temperature (you can test this by placing your hand on the bottom of the mixing bowl) and is quite shiny and airy, 5 to 7 minutes. Add the vanilla and whisk for 1 minute more.

Refrigerate the clean bowl of the stand mixer and the whisk attachment (or a medium metal bowl and beaters from a hand mixer) until quite cold, about 15 minutes.

Once chilled, remove the bowl and whisk from the refrigerator, add the cream, and whip it on medium speed until just thickened.

Increase the speed to medium-high and whip the cream until it holds stiff peaks that stand upright when the whisk is raised (the stiffer the cream, the more support it will provide the crackers in your cake).

Gently fold the marshmallow cream into the whipped cream, being mindful not to deflate the cream; it's okay to leave fluffy morsels of marshmallow throughout. Use it immediately.

Lightly coat the sides of your springform pan with cooking spray, and line the sides of the pan with a 3-by-29-in/7.5-by-75-cm strip of parchment paper. Using a small offset spatula or the back of a spoon, spread a generous layer of the whipped cream on the bottom of the pan.

Cover as much of the whipped cream as possible with a layer of the graham crackers, filling any gaps with broken crackers. The pieces should touch. The goal is a solid layer of Graham crackers.

Generously spread some of the pudding over the crackers.

Continue layering in this order (whipped cream, graham crackers, pudding, graham crackers) until you run out or reach the top of the pan. Spread the top of the cake with a final layer of whipped cream and gently cover it with plastic wrap. Refrigerate for 24 hours.

Peel the plastic wrap from the cake and run a paring knife between the paper and the pan. Open the clamp, remove the pan sides, and gently peel back the parchment paper. Transfer the cake, still on the pan bottom, to a serving platter. Sprinkle crushed graham crackers or grated chocolate on top of the cake. Using a knife, slice into wedges and serve.

PEANUT BUTTER CUP

YIELD: 15 TO 20 SERVINGS

This is our version of a large Reese's Peanut Butter Cup, and a tribute to our fanatical love of the combination of peanut butter and chocolate.

One 9-by-3-in/23-by-7.5-cm springform pan

PEANUT BUTTER PUDDING

MAKES ABOUT 6 CUPS/1.3 KG

1⅓ cups/265 g granulated sugar

6 Tbsp/50 g cornstarch

1 tsp salt

3½ cups/840 ml whole milk

1 cup/240 ml heavy cream

2 eggs, lightly beaten

¾ cup/195 g creamy peanut butter, at room temperature

2 Tbsp unsalted butter, at room temperature

1 Tbsp pure vanilla extract

PEANUT BUTTER WHIPPED CREAM

MAKES ABOUT 1 QT/800 G

2 cups/480 ml heavy cream

⅓ cup/85 g creamy peanut butter, at room temperature

¼ cup/35 g confectioners' sugar

1 tsp pure vanilla extract

ONE RECIPE GRAHAM CRACKERS

(PAGE 37)

ONE RECIPE MILK CHOCOLATE GANACHE

(PAGE 62)

Chopped chocolate-covered peanut butter cups or salted roasted peanuts for decorating

MAKE *the* PUDDING

In a large saucepan, combine the granulated sugar, cornstarch, and salt. Add the milk and cream and whisk to combine. Add the eggs, whisk again, and place the saucepan over medium-high heat, whisking constantly.

Once the mixture begins to thicken and bubbles begin popping on the surface, turn the heat to medium and whisk vigorously for 45 seconds. Remove the pan from the heat.

If the pudding has any lumps, strain it through a medium-mesh wire sieve into a heatproof bowl. Add the peanut butter, butter, and vanilla and whisk until they are incorporated.

The pudding should be used almost immediately; it should still be warm and relatively pourable when you layer it with the crackers.

MAKE *the* WHIPPED CREAM

Refrigerate the bowl of a stand mixer and the whisk attachment (or a medium metal bowl and beaters from a hand mixer) until quite cold, about 15 minutes.

Once chilled, remove the bowl and whisk from the refrigerator, add the cream, and whip it on medium speed until just thickened.

Add the peanut butter, confectioners' sugar, and vanilla and, on medium-high speed, whip the cream until it holds stiff peaks that stand upright when the whisk is raised. Use it immediately.

Lightly coat the sides of your springform pan with cooking spray, and line the sides of the pan with a 3-by-29-in/7.5-by-75-cm strip of parchment paper. Using a small offset spatula or the back of a spoon, spread a generous layer of the pudding on the bottom of the pan.

Cover as much of the pudding as possible with a layer of the graham crackers, filling any gaps with broken crackers. The pieces should touch. The goal is a solid layer of crackers.

Generously spread a layer of the ganache over the crackers.

Continue layering in this order (pudding, graham crackers, ganache) until you run out or reach the top of the pan. Spread the whipped cream on top of the cake. Gently cover the cake with plastic wrap, place it on a platter (to protect the inside of your refrigerator from any escaping ganache while the cake sets up), and refrigerate for 24 hours. (If you want to frost the sides of the cake with whipped cream as pictured on page 77, prepare the whipped cream after the cake sets up for 24 hours, and frost the top and sides just prior to serving.)

Peel the plastic wrap from the cake and run a paring knife between the paper and the pan. Open the clamp, remove the pan sides, and gently peel back the parchment paper. Transfer the cake, still on the pan bottom, to a serving platter. Decorate with chopped chocolate-covered peanut butter cups or roasted, salted peanuts. Using a knife, slice into wedges and serve.

MARSHMALLOW– PEANUT BUTTER

YIELD: 15 TO 20 SERVINGS

 White bread + peanut butter + a thick layer of marshmallow = a sandwich everyone loves. Here it is as an icebox cake, where peanut butter wafers serve as the bread, sandwiching layers of two different, yet equally delicious, whipped creams.

One 9-by-3-in/23-by-7.5-cm springform pan

PEANUT BUTTER WAFERS

MAKES ABOUT SIXTY 2¼-IN/5.5-CM WAFERS

2 cups/270 g all-purpose flour

½ tsp salt

1¼ cups/250 g granulated sugar

¾ cup/170 g unsalted butter, at room temperature

1 Tbsp pure vanilla extract

2 Tbsp whole milk

1 Tbsp light corn syrup

1 cup/260 g creamy peanut butter, at room temperature

ONE RECIPE MARSHMALLOW– CREAM WHIPPED CREAM

(PAGE 72)

ONE RECIPE PEANUT BUTTER WHIPPED CREAM

(PAGE 76)

Chopped roasted, salted peanuts for decorating

→

MAKE *the* WAFERS

In a medium bowl, whisk together the flour and salt.

In the bowl of a stand mixer fitted with the paddle attachment, cream the granulated sugar, butter, and vanilla on medium-low speed until slightly fluffy, about 2 minutes. Be careful not to overbeat. Scrape the sides of the bowl with a rubber spatula.

In a small bowl, whisk the milk and corn syrup to combine. Add the milk mixture to the butter-sugar mixture with the mixer on medium-low speed; beat until just combined. Scrape the sides of the bowl with the rubber spatula. Add the peanut butter and beat until incorporated.

Add the flour mixture all at once to the mixer bowl. With the mixer on low speed, beat until the dough just begins to pull away from the bottom of the bowl and forms a cohesive mass. Scrape the sides of the bowl to fully incorporate all the ingredients.

Divide the dough in half and place each half on a sheet of plastic wrap. Loosely wrap the dough and form each half into a log about 2 in/5 cm wide. Roll the logs along the counter, still wrapped in plastic wrap, in order to shape into perfect cylinders. Tighten the plastic wrap around the logs and freeze them for at least 2 hours, or overnight. If you have trouble forming the soft dough into logs, form the dough into a disk (or loose log shape), wrap it in plastic wrap, and place in the freezer for about 20 minutes, just until it is cold enough to shape into the necessary log. Line two baking sheets with parchment paper.

Once frozen, unwrap one of the logs and use a sharp paring or chef's knife to cut it into thin slices about ⅛ in/3 mm thick; rotate the log as you slice, or the side sitting on the cutting surface will flatten. Arrange the slices about 1 in/2.5 cm apart on one of the prepared baking sheets and place in the freezer for at least 10 minutes. Repeat with the second dough log and prepared baking sheet. If you need more room to fit all your dough slices, simply arrange them on additional sheets of parchment paper, layer the dough-covered papers one on top of the other on the second baking sheet in the freezer, and switch them out as you bake off each batch. (You can also wrap the baking sheets in plastic wrap and freeze the rounds for up to 1 week.)

Position a rack in the center of the oven and preheat to 350°F/180°C.

Place one baking sheet of the frozen dough rounds in the oven and bake until they begin to brown just around the edges, 10 to 12 minutes, rotating the sheet halfway through the baking time. Using a stiff metal or plastic spatula, immediately press down lightly on each cookie to flatten it. Let the wafers cool on the baking sheet for 2 to 3 minutes, then transfer them to a wire rack to cool completely. The wafers should be very crispy when cooled. If they are not, place them back in the 350°F/180°C oven for 1 to 2 minutes more. Repeat to bake the additional sheets of frozen dough rounds.

Store the wafers in an airtight container as soon as they have cooled. They will remain crispy at room temperature, tightly sealed, for about 24 hours. Freezing the baked wafers in a resealable plastic bag also works well, for up to 1 month. There is no need to defrost the wafers before assembling your cake.

Keep in mind that this cake has two flavors of whipped cream layered throughout. Lightly coat the sides of your springform pan with cooking spray, and line the sides of the pan with a 3-by-29-in/7.5-by-75-cm strip of parchment paper. Using a small offset spatula or the back of a spoon, spread a generous layer of the marshmallow whipped cream on the bottom of the pan.

Cover as much of the whipped cream as possible with a layer of the wafers, filling any gaps with broken wafers. The pieces should touch. The goal is a solid layer of wafers.

Generously spread some of the peanut butter whipped cream over the wafers, then add another layer of wafers on top.

Continue layering in this order (marshmallow whipped cream, wafers, peanut butter whipped cream, wafers) until you run out or reach the top of the pan. The final layer of the cake should be whipped cream (either flavor is fine). Gently cover the cake in plastic wrap. Refrigerate for 24 hours.

Peel the plastic wrap from the cake and run a paring knife between the paper and the pan. Open the clamp, remove the pan sides, and gently peel back the parchment paper. Transfer the cake, still on the pan bottom, to a serving platter. Sprinkle chopped peanuts around the perimeter of the top of the cake. Using a knife, slice into wedges and serve.

THE KING

We know Elvis was on to something with his love of peanut butter and bananas. We added chocolate to this mix to send it off the charts.

One 8-by-8-by-2-in/20-by-20-by-5-cm square baking pan

THE KING PEANUT BUTTER PUDDING

MAKES ABOUT 5 CUPS/1 KG

1 cup/200 g granulated sugar

¼ cup/35 g cornstarch

¾ tsp salt

2½ cups/600 ml whole milk

¾ cup/180 ml heavy cream

1 egg, lightly beaten

Rounded ½ cup/145 g creamy peanut butter, at room temperature

1 Tbsp unsalted butter, at room temperature

2 tsp pure vanilla extract

THE KING PEANUT BUTTER WHIPPED CREAM

MAKES ABOUT 3 CUPS/425 G

1½ cups/360 ml heavy cream

¼ cup/65 g creamy peanut butter, at room temperature

3 Tbsp confectioners' sugar

¾ tsp pure vanilla extract

ONE RECIPE CHOCOLATE GRAHAM CRACKERS

(PAGE 66)

8 nicely ripened bananas; 6 sliced lengthwise into 5 slices, 2 cut into rounds for decorating

→

MAKE the PUDDING

In a medium saucepan, combine the granulated sugar, cornstarch, and salt. Add the milk and cream and whisk to combine. Add the egg, whisk again, and place the saucepan over medium-high heat, whisking constantly.

Once the mixture begins to thicken and bubbles begin popping on the surface, turn the heat to medium and whisk vigorously for 45 seconds. Remove the pan from the heat.

If the pudding has any lumps, strain it through a medium-mesh wire sieve into a heatproof bowl. Add the peanut butter, butter, and vanilla and whisk until they are incorporated.

The pudding should be used almost immediately; it should still be warm and relatively pourable when you layer it with the crackers.

MAKE the WHIPPED CREAM

Refrigerate the bowl of a stand mixer and the whisk attachment (or a medium metal bowl and beaters from a hand mixer) until quite cold, about 15 minutes.

Once chilled, remove the bowl and whisk from the refrigerator, add the cream, and whip it on medium speed until just thickened.

Add the peanut butter, confectioners' sugar, and vanilla and, on medium-high speed, whip the cream until it holds stiff peaks that stand upright when the whisk is raised. Use it immediately.

Using a small offset spatula or the back of a spoon, spread a generous layer of the pudding on the bottom of the baking pan.

Cover as much of the pudding as possible with a layer of the graham crackers, filling any gaps with broken crackers. The pieces should touch. The goal is a solid layer of graham crackers.

Place a thin layer of banana slices over the crackers.

Continue layering in this order (pudding, crackers, bananas) until you run out or reach the top of the pan. Spread the top of the cake with the whipped cream and gently cover it with plastic wrap. Refrigerate for 24 hours.

Peel the plastic wrap from the cake and top the cake with the banana rounds. Serve portions directly from the pan.

BANANA-RUM

YIELD: 9 TO 12 SERVINGS

We think it would be unfair to write a book about icebox cakes and not give a grateful nod to banana cream pie. Our icebox version substitutes graham crackers for the pie crust, and separates the bananas from the pudding, giving each a hearty glug of rum. Finally, we caramelize the bananas, which may just bring banana pie devotees to their knees.

One 8-by-8-by-2-in/20-by-20-by-5-cm square baking pan

CARAMELIZED RUM BANANAS

MAKES ABOUT 2 CUPS/560 G

6 Tbsp/85 g unsalted butter

6 nicely ripened bananas, cut into ½-in/12-mm rounds

6 Tbsp/90 g packed dark brown sugar

½ tsp salt

½ cup/120 ml dark rum

VANILLA-RUM PUDDING

MAKES ABOUT 5 CUPS/1 KG

1 cup/200 g granulated sugar

¼ cup/35 g cornstarch

¾ tsp salt

2½ cups/600 ml whole milk

¾ cup/180 ml heavy cream

1 egg, lightly beaten

¼ cup/60 ml dark rum, or to taste

1 Tbsp unsalted butter, at room temperature

2 tsp pure vanilla extract

→

VANILLA-RUM WHIPPED CREAM

MAKES ABOUT 3 CUPS/420 G

1½ cups/360 ml heavy cream

¼ cup/60 ml dark rum

3 Tbsp confectioners' sugar

½ tsp pure vanilla extract

ONE RECIPE GRAHAM CRACKERS

(PAGE 37)

Chopped bananas for decorating

MAKE *the* CARAMELIZED BANANAS

Melt the butter in a large skillet over medium-high heat until the foam subsides. Add the bananas and cook, flipping them over to ensure they begin to brown on both sides.

Once the bananas have browned and softened up a bit, add the brown sugar and salt and continue cooking the bananas for 1 or 2 minutes more so their color darkens and the sugar melts.

Add the rum and cook until the sauce thickens again, about 2 minutes. Remove the pan from the heat and allow the bananas to cool to room temperature. They are best used the same day.

MAKE *the* PUDDING

In a medium saucepan, combine the granulated sugar, cornstarch, and salt. Add the milk and cream and whisk to combine. Add the egg, whisk again, and place the saucepan over medium-high heat, whisking constantly.

Once the mixture begins to thicken and bubbles begin popping on the surface, turn the heat to medium and whisk vigorously for 45 seconds. Remove the pan from the heat.

If the pudding has any lumps, strain it through a medium-mesh wire sieve into a heatproof bowl. Add the rum, butter, and vanilla and whisk until they are incorporated.

The pudding should be used almost immediately; it should still be warm and relatively pourable when you layer it with the crackers.

MAKE *the* WHIPPED CREAM

Refrigerate the bowl of a stand mixer and the whisk attachment (or a medium metal bowl and beaters from a hand mixer) until quite cold, about 15 minutes.

Once chilled, remove the bowl and whisk from the refrigerator, add the cream, and whip it on medium speed until just thickened.

Add the rum, confectioners' sugar, and vanilla and, on medium-high speed, whip the cream until it holds stiff peaks that stand upright when the whisk is raised. Use it immediately.

Using a small offset spatula or the back of a spoon, spread a generous layer of the pudding on the bottom of the baking pan.

Cover as much of the pudding as possible with a layer of the graham crackers, filling any gaps with broken crackers. The pieces should touch. The goal is a solid layer of graham crackers.

Layer some of the caramelized bananas over the crackers.

Continue layering in this order (pudding, crackers, bananas) until you run out or reach the top of the pan. Spread the top of the cake with the whipped cream and gently cover it with plastic wrap. Refrigerate for 24 hours.

Peel the plastic wrap from the cake and top the cake with chopped bananas. Serve portions directly from the pan.

BLACK PEPPER-RUM

This icebox cake pays homage to the Triple Rum Black Pepper Cake from *Baked Elements*, by Matt Lewis and Renato Poliafito. Jessie tested and developed many of the recipes for Matt and Renato's book, and she fell hard for the flavors in this particular cake. Who would have thought that freshly ground black pepper and rum would pair so beautifully? (You'll have extra wafers left over after assembling your cake—lucky you! Store them in a resealable plastic bag in the freezer and enjoy them for up to 1 month.)

One 9-by-5-by-3-in/23-by-12-by-7.5-cm
loaf pan

One 10-in/25-cm oval or rectangular
serving platter

BLACK PEPPER WAFERS

MAKES ABOUT SIXTY
2¼-IN/5.5-CM WAFERS

2 cups/270 g all-purpose flour

1½ Tbsp freshly ground black pepper

¾ tsp salt

1¼ cups/250 g granulated sugar

¾ cup/170 g unsalted butter,
at room temperature

1 Tbsp pure vanilla extract

2 Tbsp whole milk

1 Tbsp light corn syrup

RUM-BLACK PEPPER WHIPPED CREAM

MAKES ABOUT 6 CUPS/780 G

3 cups/720 ml heavy cream

⅓ cup/45 g confectioners' sugar

¼ cup/60 ml dark rum

2 tsp freshly ground black pepper

Crushed Black Pepper Wafers
and freshly ground black pepper
for decorating

→

MAKE *the* WAFERS

In a medium bowl, whisk together the flour, pepper, and salt.

In the bowl of a stand mixer fitted with the paddle attachment, cream the granulated sugar, butter, and vanilla on medium-low speed until slightly fluffy, about 2 minutes. Be careful not to overbeat. Scrape the sides of the bowl with a rubber spatula.

In a small bowl, whisk the milk and corn syrup to combine. Add the milk mixture to the butter-sugar mixture with the mixer on medium-low speed; beat until just combined. Scrape the sides of the bowl with the rubber spatula.

Add the flour mixture all at once to the mixer bowl. With the mixer on low speed, beat until the dough just begins to pull away from the bottom of the bowl and forms a cohesive mass. Scrape the sides of the bowl to fully incorporate all the ingredients.

Divide the dough in half and place each half on a sheet of plastic wrap. Loosely wrap the dough and form each half into a log about 2 in/5 cm wide. Roll the logs along the counter, still wrapped in plastic wrap, in order to shape into perfect cylinders. Tighten the plastic wrap around the logs and freeze them for at least 2 hours, or overnight. If you have trouble forming the soft dough into logs, form the dough into a disk (or loose log shape), wrap it in plastic wrap, and place in the freezer for about 20 minutes, just until it is cold enough to shape into the necessary log. Line two baking sheets with parchment paper.

Once frozen, unwrap one of the logs and use a sharp paring or chef's knife to cut it into thin slices about ⅛ in/3 mm thick; rotate the log as you slice, or the side sitting on the cutting surface will flatten. Arrange the slices about 1 in/2.5 cm apart on one of the prepared baking sheets and place in the freezer for at least 10 minutes. Repeat with the second dough log and prepared baking sheet. If you need more room to fit all your dough slices, simply arrange them on additional sheets of parchment paper, layer the dough-covered papers one on top of the other on the second baking sheet in the freezer, and switch them out as you bake off each batch. (You can also wrap the baking sheets in plastic wrap and freeze the rounds for up to 1 week.)

Position a rack in the center of the oven and preheat to 350°F/180°C.

Place one baking sheet of the frozen dough rounds in the oven and bake until they begin to brown just around the edges, 10 to 12 minutes, rotating the sheet halfway through the baking time. Using a stiff metal or plastic spatula, immediately press down lightly on each cookie to flatten it. Let the wafers cool on the baking sheet for 2 to 3 minutes, then transfer them to a wire rack to cool completely. The wafers should be very crispy when cooled. If they are not, place them back in the 350°F/180°C oven for 1 to 2 minutes more. Repeat to bake the additional sheets of frozen dough rounds.

Store the wafers in an airtight container as soon as they have cooled. They will remain crispy at room temperature, tightly sealed, for about 24 hours. Freezing the baked wafers in a resealable plastic bag also works well, for up to 1 month. There is no need to defrost the wafers before assembling your cake.

MAKE *the* WHIPPED CREAM

Refrigerate the bowl of a stand mixer and the whisk attachment (or a medium metal bowl and beaters from a hand mixer) until quite cold, about 15 minutes.

Once chilled, remove the bowl and whisk from the refrigerator, add the cream, and whip it on medium speed until just thickened.

Add the confectioners' sugar, rum, and pepper and, on medium-high speed, whip the cream until it holds stiff peaks that stand upright when the whisk is raised (the stiffer the cream, the more support it will provide the wafers in your cake). Use it immediately.

Line the loaf pan with plastic wrap that hangs slightly over the pan sides. Using a small offset spatula or the back of a spoon, spread a generous layer of the whipped cream on the bottom of the lined pan.

Cover as much of the whipped cream as possible with a layer of the wafers, filling any gaps with broken wafers. The pieces should touch. The goal is a solid layer of wafers.

Continue layering whipped cream and wafers until you run out or reach the top of the pan, ending with whipped cream. Gently cover the cake with plastic wrap. Refrigerate for 24 hours.

Peel the plastic wrap from the cake, place the serving platter over the cake, and invert the cake onto the platter. Carefully remove the pan and plastic-wrap lining and sprinkle crushed black pepper wafers and freshly ground black pepper on top of the cake. Using a knife, cut it into slices and serve.

CHAI-GINGER

YIELD: 15 TO 20 SERVINGS

 This cake was created for the chilly days of fall and winter, when you're just the tiniest bit tired of chocolate (sacrilege, we know) and when locally grown fruit is no longer an option. It combines the warm spices of the harvest season and is a tasty, yet sophisticated, alternative to pumpkin pie.

One 9-by-3-in/23-by-7.5-cm springform pan

GINGER WAFERS

MAKES ABOUT SIXTY
2¼-IN/5.5-CM WAFERS

2 cups/270 g all-purpose flour

2 Tbsp ground ginger

1 tsp ground cinnamon

½ tsp ground nutmeg

¼ tsp ground cloves

½ tsp salt

1¼ cups/250 g granulated sugar

¾ cup/170 g unsalted butter, at room temperature

2 Tbsp whole milk

1 Tbsp light corn syrup

CHAI WHIPPED CREAM

MAKES ABOUT 8 CUPS/1 KG

1 qt/960 ml heavy cream

½ cup/65 g confectioners' sugar

¼ cup/60 ml bourbon, or to taste

1½ Tbsp pure vanilla extract

2 tsp ground cardamom

1½ tsp ground ginger

1 tsp ground cinnamon

½ tsp ground cloves

½ tsp ground nutmeg

½ tsp ground allspice

ONE RECIPE SALTY CARAMEL

(PAGE 66)

Ground cinnamon for decorating

→

MAKE *the* WAFERS

In a medium bowl, whisk together the flour, ginger, cinnamon, nutmeg, cloves, and salt.

In the bowl of a stand mixer fitted with the paddle attachment, cream the granulated sugar and butter on medium-low speed until slightly fluffy, about 2 minutes. Be careful not to overbeat. Scrape the sides of the bowl with a rubber spatula.

In a small bowl, whisk the milk and corn syrup to combine. Add the milk mixture to the butter-sugar mixture with the mixer on medium-low speed; beat until just combined. Scrape the sides of the bowl with the rubber spatula.

Add the flour mixture all at once to the mixer bowl. With the mixer on low speed, beat until the dough just begins to pull away from the bottom of the bowl and forms a cohesive mass. Scrape the sides of the bowl to fully incorporate all the ingredients.

Divide the dough in half and place each half on a sheet of plastic wrap. Loosely wrap the dough and form each half into a log about 2 in/5 cm wide. Roll the logs along the counter, still wrapped in plastic wrap, in order to shape into perfect cylinders. Tighten the plastic wrap around the logs and freeze them for at least 2 hours, or overnight. If you have trouble forming the soft dough into logs, form the dough into a disk (or loose log shape), wrap it in plastic wrap, and place in the freezer for about 20 minutes, just until it is cold enough to shape into the necessary log. Line two baking sheets with parchment paper.

Once frozen, unwrap one of the logs and use a sharp paring or chef's knife to cut it into thin slices about ⅛ in/3 mm thick; rotate the log as you slice, or the side sitting on the cutting surface will flatten. Arrange the slices about 1 in/2.5 cm apart on one of the prepared baking sheets and place in the freezer for at least 10 minutes. Repeat with the second dough log and prepared baking sheet. If you need more room to fit all your dough slices, simply arrange them on additional sheets of parchment paper, layer the dough-covered papers one on top of the other on the second baking sheet in the freezer, and switch them out as you bake off each batch. (You can also wrap the baking sheets in plastic wrap and freeze the rounds for up to 1 week.)

Position a rack in the center of the oven and preheat to 350°F/180°C.

Place one baking sheet of the frozen dough rounds in the oven and bake until they begin to brown just around the edges, 10 to 12 minutes, rotating the sheet halfway through the baking time. Using a stiff metal or plastic spatula, immediately press down lightly on each cookie to flatten it. Let the wafers cool on the baking sheet for 2 to 3 minutes, then transfer them to a wire rack to cool completely. The wafers should be very crispy when cooled. If they are not, place them back in the 350°F/180°C oven for 1 to 2 minutes more. Repeat to bake the additional sheets of frozen dough rounds.

Store the wafers in an airtight container as soon as they have cooled. They will remain crispy at room temperature, tightly sealed, for about 24 hours. Freezing the baked wafers in a resealable plastic bag also works well, for up to 1 month. There is no need to defrost the wafers before assembling your cake.

MAKE *the* WHIPPED CREAM

Refrigerate the bowl of a stand mixer and the whisk attachment (or a medium metal bowl and beaters from a hand mixer) until quite cold, about 15 minutes.

Once chilled, remove the bowl and whisk from the refrigerator, add the cream, and whip it on medium speed until just thickened.

Add the confectioners' sugar, bourbon, vanilla, and spices and, on medium-high speed, whip the cream until it holds stiff peaks that stand upright when the whisk is raised (the stiffer the cream, the more support it will provide the wafers in your cake). Use it immediately.

Lightly coat the sides of your springform pan with cooking spray, and line the sides of the pan with a 3-by-29-in/7.5-by-75-cm strip of parchment paper. Using a small offset spatula or the back of a spoon, spread a generous layer of the whipped cream on the bottom of the pan.

Cover as much of the whipped cream as possible with a layer of the wafers, filling any gaps with broken wafers. The pieces should touch. The goal is a solid layer of wafers.

Generously spread a layer of the caramel over the wafers.

Continue layering in this order (whipped cream, wafers, caramel) until you run out or reach the top of the pan. Spread the top of the cake with a final layer of whipped cream and gently cover it with plastic wrap. Refrigerate for 24 hours.

Peel the plastic wrap from the cake and run a paring knife between the paper and the pan. Open the clamp, remove the pan sides, and gently peel back the parchment paper. Transfer the cake, still on the pan bottom, to a serving platter. Lightly dust cinnamon on top of the cake. Using a knife, slice into wedges and serve.

RASPBERRY GANACHE

YIELD: 9 TO 12 SERVINGS

This cake is a throwback to the 1980s, when raspberry purée was all the rage and frequently dribbled on chocolate desserts. Here, we turn this classic pairing on its head, incorporating the purée into the pudding and whipped cream, making for two very fruity additions. And, of course, there's chocolate in its most luxurious form: Ganache.

One 8-by-8-by-2-in/20-by-20-by-5-cm square baking pan

DARK CHOCOLATE GANACHE

MAKES ABOUT 1 CUP/350 G

9 oz/255 g dark chocolate (60 to 70 percent cacao), finely chopped

¾ cup/180 ml heavy cream

RASPBERRY PUDDING

MAKES ABOUT 5 CUPS/1 KG

1 cup/200 g granulated sugar

¼ cup/35 g cornstarch

¾ tsp salt

2½ cups/600 ml whole milk

¾ cup/180 ml heavy cream

1 egg, lightly beaten

½ cup/120 ml Raspberry Purée (recipe follows)

1 Tbsp unsalted butter, at room temperature

1¼ tsp raspberry extract, or to taste

2 to 3 drops red food coloring (optional)

→

RASPBERRY WHIPPED CREAM

MAKES ABOUT 3 CUPS/480 G

1½ cups/360 ml heavy cream

½ cup/120 ml Raspberry Purée
(recipe follows)

3 Tbsp confectioners' sugar

¾ tsp raspberry extract, or to taste

ONE RECIPE LADYFINGERS

(PAGE 54)

Fresh raspberries for decorating

MAKE the GANACHE

Place the chocolate in a medium heatproof bowl and set aside. In a small saucepan, heat the cream over medium-high heat just until bubbles begin to form around the edges.

Pour the warm cream over the chocolate and let sit for 1 minute so it begins to melt. Gently whisk until fully incorporated and shiny.

Let come to room temperature, stirring occasionally, until it thickens and is less like chocolate syrup and pours more like hot fudge.

(To make ahead, let cool to room temperature, cover, and refrigerate for up to 1 week. Reheat it over medium-low heat until liquefied.)

MAKE the PUDDING

In a medium saucepan, combine the granulated sugar, cornstarch, and salt. Add the milk and cream and whisk to combine. Add the egg, whisk again, and place the saucepan over medium-high heat, whisking constantly.

Once the mixture begins to thicken and bubbles begin popping on the surface, turn the heat to medium and whisk vigorously for 45 seconds. Remove the pan from the heat.

If the pudding has any lumps, strain it through a medium-mesh wire sieve into a heatproof bowl. Add the raspberry purée, butter, raspberry extract, and food coloring (if using) and whisk until they are incorporated.

The pudding should be used almost immediately; it should still be warm and relatively pourable when you layer it with the ladyfingers.

MAKE *the* WHIPPED CREAM

Refrigerate the bowl of a stand mixer and the whisk attachment (or a medium metal bowl and beaters from a hand mixer) until quite cold, about 15 minutes.

Once chilled, remove the bowl and whisk from the refrigerator, add the cream, and whip it on medium speed until just thickened.

Add the raspberry purée, confectioners' sugar, and raspberry extract and, on medium-high speed, whip the cream until it holds stiff peaks that stand upright when the whisk is raised. Use it immediately.

Using a small offset spatula or the back of a spoon, spread a generous layer of the pudding on the bottom of the baking pan.

Cover as much of the pudding as possible with a layer of the ladyfingers, filling any gaps with broken ladyfingers. The pieces should touch. The goal is a solid layer of ladyfingers.

Generously spread a layer of the ganache over the ladyfingers.

Continue layering in this order (pudding, ladyfingers, ganache) until you run out or reach the top of the pan. Spread the top of the cake with the whipped cream and gently cover it with plastic wrap. Refrigerate for 24 hours.

Peel the plastic wrap from the cake and scatter fresh raspberries on top of the cake. Serve portions directly from the pan and drizzle them with some of the remaining purée.

RASPBERRY PURÉE

In a small saucepan, combine 3 cups/370 g fresh raspberries, ½ cup/100 g granulated sugar, 1 to 2 Tbsp fresh lemon juice, and ¼ tsp salt over medium-high heat and cook, mashing and stirring the berries with a wooden spoon or heatproof rubber spatula, until the raspberries are broken up and the mixture is soupy, about 3 minutes. Remove the pan from the heat and let the purée cool briefly.

Strain the purée through a medium-mesh wire sieve into a heatproof bowl, working the purée through with a wooden spoon or rubber spatula. Let cool to room temperature before using.

The purée will keep covered tightly in the refrigerator for up to 1 week.

MAKES ABOUT 1¼ CUPS/300 ML

LAVENDER-BLUEBERRY

This cake was conceived after Jessie enjoyed many lavender shortbread cookies one summer. The subtle floral flavor of lavender melds brilliantly with the fruity richness of blueberry whipped cream. (You'll have extra wafers left over after assembling your cake—lucky you! Store them in a resealable plastic bag in the freezer and enjoy them for up to 1 month.)

One 9-by-5-by-3-in/23-by-12-by-7.5-cm loaf pan

One 10-in/25-cm oval or rectangular serving platter

LAVENDER WAFERS

MAKES ABOUT SIXTY
2¼-IN/5.5-CM WAFERS

2 cups/270 g all-purpose flour

2 Tbsp culinary lavender (see box, page 106)

½ tsp salt

1¼ cups/250 g granulated sugar

¾ cup/170 g unsalted butter, at room temperature

1 Tbsp pure vanilla extract

2 Tbsp whole milk

1 Tbsp light corn syrup

BLUEBERRY WHIPPED CREAM

MAKES ABOUT 6 CUPS/1.1 KG

3 cups/720 ml heavy cream

1 cup/325 g Blueberry Compote (recipe follows), whisked

⅓ cup/45 g confectioners' sugar

Fresh blueberries for decorating

→

MAKE *the* WAFERS

In a medium bowl, whisk together the flour, lavender, and salt.

In the bowl of a stand mixer fitted with the paddle attachment, cream the granulated sugar, butter, and vanilla on medium-low speed until slightly fluffy, about 2 minutes. Be careful not to overbeat. Scrape the sides of the bowl with a rubber spatula.

In a small bowl, whisk the milk and corn syrup to combine. Add the milk mixture to the butter-sugar mixture with the mixer on medium-low speed; beat until just combined. Scrape the sides of the bowl with the rubber spatula.

Add the flour mixture all at once to the mixer bowl. With the mixer on low speed, beat until the dough just begins to pull away from the bottom of the bowl and forms a cohesive mass. Scrape the sides of the bowl to fully incorporate all the ingredients.

Divide the dough in half and place each half on a sheet of plastic wrap. Loosely wrap the dough and form each half into a log about 2 in/5 cm wide. Roll the logs along the counter, still wrapped in plastic wrap, in order to shape into perfect cylinders. Tighten the plastic wrap around the logs and freeze them for at least 2 hours, or overnight. If you have trouble forming the soft dough into logs, form the dough into a disk (or loose log shape), wrap it in plastic wrap, and place in the freezer for about 20 minutes, just until it is cold enough to shape into the necessary log. Line two baking sheets with parchment paper.

Once frozen, unwrap one of the logs and use a sharp paring or chef's knife to cut it into thin slices about ⅛ in/3 mm thick; rotate the log as you slice, or the side sitting on the cutting surface will flatten. Arrange the slices about 1 in/2.5 cm apart on one of the prepared baking sheets and place in the freezer for at least 10 minutes. Repeat with the second dough log and prepared baking sheet. If you need more room to fit all your dough slices, simply arrange them on additional sheets of parchment paper, layer the dough-covered papers one on top of the other on the second baking sheet in the freezer, and switch them out as you bake off each batch. (You can also wrap the baking sheets in plastic wrap and freeze the rounds for up to 1 week.)

Position a rack in the center of the oven and preheat to 350°F/180°C.

Place one baking sheet of the frozen dough rounds in the oven and bake until they begin to brown just around the edges, 10 to 12 minutes, rotating the sheet halfway through the baking time. Using a stiff metal or plastic spatula, immediately press down lightly on each cookie to flatten it. Let the wafers cool on the baking sheet for 2 to 3 minutes, then transfer them to a wire rack to cool completely. The wafers should be very crispy when cooled. If they are not, place them back in the 350°F/180°C oven for 1 to 2 minutes more. Repeat to bake the additional sheets of frozen dough rounds.

Store the wafers in an airtight container as soon as they have cooled. They will remain crispy at room temperature, tightly sealed, for about 24 hours. Freezing the baked wafers in a resealable plastic bag also works well, for up to 1 month. There is no need to defrost the wafers before assembling your cake.

MAKE *the* WHIPPED CREAM

Refrigerate the bowl of a stand mixer and the whisk attachment (or a medium metal bowl and beaters from a hand mixer) until quite cold, about 15 minutes.

Once chilled, remove the bowl and whisk from the refrigerator, add the cream, and whip it on medium speed until it is just thickened.

Add the blueberry compote and confectioners' sugar and, on medium-high speed, whip the cream until it holds stiff peaks that stand upright when the whisk is raised (the stiffer the cream, the more support it will provide the wafers in your cake). Use it immediately.

Line the loaf pan with plastic wrap that hangs slightly over the pan sides. Using a small offset spatula or the back of a spoon, spread a generous layer of the whipped cream on the bottom of the lined pan.

Cover as much of the whipped cream as possible with a layer of the wafers, filling any gaps with broken wafers. The pieces should touch. The goal is a solid layer of wafers.

Continue layering whipped cream and wafers until you run out or reach the top of the pan, ending with whipped cream. Gently cover it with plastic wrap. Refrigerate for 24 hours.

Peel the plastic wrap from the cake, place the serving platter over the cake, and invert the cake onto the platter. Carefully remove the pan and plastic-wrap lining and sprinkle fresh blueberries on top of the cake. Using a knife, cut it into slices and serve.

BLUEBERRY COMPOTE

In a small saucepan, combine 3 cups/445 g fresh blueberries, ⅓ cup/65 g granulated sugar, 3 Tbsp lemon juice, and ¼ tsp salt over medium heat. Cook, uncovered and stirring frequently, until the mixture reduces to a generous 1 cup/ 240 ml, 25 to 30 minutes. The mixture should be simmering but not vigorously boiling. Once reduced, the compote will be quite thick. Let cool to room temperature before using. The compote will keep tightly covered in the refrigerator for up to 1 week.

MAKES ABOUT 1 CUP/325 G

KEY LIME PIE

YIELD: 12 TO 15 SERVINGS

This icebox cake gives you all of the tangy, citrusy creaminess of a Key lime pie, with a little coconut thrown in for good measure. This is a quintessential summertime dessert. (You'll have extra wafers left over after assembling your cake—lucky you! Store them in a resealable plastic bag in the freezer and enjoy them for up to 1 month.)

One 9-by-5-by-3-in/23-by-12-by-7.5-cm loaf pan

One 10-in/25-cm oval or rectangular serving platter

KEY LIME WAFERS

MAKES ABOUT SIXTY
2¼-IN/5.5-CM WAFERS

2¼ cups/305 g all-purpose flour

½ tsp salt

¼ cup/20 g finely grated Key lime or Persian lime zest (see box, page 45)

1¼ cups/250 g granulated sugar

¾ cup/170 g unsalted butter, at room temperature

¼ cup/60 ml freshly squeezed Key lime or Persian lime juice (see box, page 45)

1 Tbsp light corn syrup

LIME-COCONUT WHIPPED CREAM

MAKES ABOUT 6 CUPS/1 KG

3 cups/720 ml heavy cream

1½ cups/240 g packed sweetened shredded coconut, toasted (see box, page 110)

½ cup/65 g confectioners' sugar

⅓ cup/30 g finely grated Key lime or Persian lime zest (see box, page 45)

¼ cup/60 ml freshly squeezed Key lime or Persian lime juice (see box, page 45)

1 Tbsp coconut extract

Ground-up or crushed graham crackers and grated lime zest for decorating

→

In a medium bowl, whisk together the flour and salt.

In the bowl of a stand mixer, use your fingers to rub the lime zest into the granulated sugar (this activates the zest and brings out its flavor). Then add the butter and cream it on medium-low speed until slightly fluffy, about 2 minutes. Be careful not to overbeat. Scrape the sides of the bowl with a rubber spatula.

In a small bowl, whisk the lime juice and corn syrup to combine. Add the juice mixture to the butter-sugar mixture with the mixer on medium-low speed; beat until just combined. Scrape the sides of the bowl with the rubber spatula.

Add the flour mixture all at once to the mixer bowl. With the mixer on low speed, beat until the dough just begins to come together. Scrape the sides of the bowl to fully incorporate all the ingredients.

Divide the dough in half and place each half on a sheet of plastic wrap. Loosely wrap the dough and form each half into a log about 2 in/ 5 cm wide. Roll the logs along the counter, still wrapped in plastic wrap, in order to shape into perfect cylinders. Tighten the plastic wrap around the logs and freeze them for at least 2 hours, or overnight. If you have trouble forming the soft dough into logs, form the dough into a disk (or loose log shape), wrap it in plastic wrap, and place in the freezer for about 20 minutes, just until it is cold enough to shape into the necessary log. Line two baking sheets with parchment paper.

TOASTING COCONUT

Place shredded coconut on a baking sheet and bake in a 350°F/180°C oven until the coconut begins to uniformly brown, 10 to 15 minutes. Stir the coconut a bit with a spatula midway through baking to ensure even browning.

Once frozen, unwrap one of the logs and use a sharp paring or chef's knife to cut it into thin slices about ⅛ in/3 mm thick; rotate the log as you slice, or the side sitting on the cutting surface will flatten. Arrange the slices about 1 in/2.5 cm apart on one of the prepared baking sheets and place in the freezer for at least 10 minutes. Repeat with the second dough log and prepared baking sheet. If you need more room to fit all your dough slices, simply arrange them on additional sheets of parchment paper, layer the dough-covered papers one on top of the other on the second baking sheet in the freezer, and switch them out as you bake off each batch. (You can also wrap the baking sheets in plastic wrap and freeze the rounds for up to 1 week.)

Position a rack in the center of the oven and preheat to 350°F/180°C.

Place one baking sheet of the frozen dough rounds in the oven and bake until they begin to brown just around the edges, 10 to 12 minutes, rotating the sheet halfway through the baking time. Using a stiff metal or plastic spatula, immediately press down lightly on each cookie to flatten it. Let the wafers cool on the baking sheet for 2 to 3 minutes, then transfer them to a wire rack to cool completely. The wafers should be very crispy when cooled. If they are not, place them back in the 350°F/180°C oven for 1 to 2 minutes more. Repeat to bake the additional sheets of dough rounds.

Store the wafers in an airtight container as soon as they have cooled. They will remain crispy at room temperature, tightly sealed, for about 24 hours. Freezing the baked wafers in a resealable plastic bag also works well, for up to 1 month. There is no need to defrost the wafers before assembling your cake.

MAKE *the* WHIPPED CREAM

Refrigerate the bowl of a stand mixer and the whisk attachment (or a medium metal bowl and beaters from a hand mixer) until quite cold, about 15 minutes.

Once chilled, remove the bowl and whisk from the refrigerator, add the cream, and whip it on medium speed until just thickened.

Add the coconut, confectioners' sugar, lime zest, lime juice, and coconut extract and, on medium-high speed, whip the cream until it holds stiff peaks that stand upright when the whisk is raised (the stiffer the cream, the more support it will provide the wafers in your cake). Use it immediately.

Line the loaf pan with plastic wrap that hangs slightly over the pan sides. Using a small offset spatula or the back of a spoon, spread a generous layer of the whipped cream on the bottom of the lined pan.

Cover as much of the whipped cream as possible with a layer of the wafers, filling any gaps with broken wafers. The pieces should touch. The goal is a solid layer of wafers.

Continue layering whipped cream and wafers until you run out or reach the top of the pan, ending with whipped cream. Gently cover it with plastic wrap. Refrigerate for 24 hours.

Peel the plastic wrap from the cake, place the serving platter over the cake, and invert the cake onto the platter. Carefully remove the pan and plastic-wrap lining and sprinkle a handful or two of graham cracker crumbs and a dusting of lime zest on top of the cake. Using a knife, cut it into slices and serve.

PERSIAN LIMES VS. KEY LIMES

In this recipe, you can substitute standard limes, also known as Persian limes, for the petite Key limes. Persian limes are easier to zest and juice—and produce more of each—than Key limes, due to their larger size, and the difference in taste is negligible.

LUSCIOUS LEMON

YIELD: 15 TO 20 SERVINGS

 Inspired by Jessie's grandmother's lemon velvet cake, the Luscious Lemon aims to capture the tart goodness of an old-fashioned lemon sheet cake, set off with just the right amount of sweet. This cake is extra special with both pudding and whipped cream layered throughout. Please note that the lemon curd needs to be prepared ahead of time, because it takes about 2 hours to set up in the refrigerator before it is added to the whipped cream.

One 9-by-3-in/23-by-7.5-cm springform pan

LEMON PUDDING

MAKES ABOUT 5 CUPS/1 KG

1 cup/200 g granulated sugar

¼ cup/35 g cornstarch

¾ tsp salt

2½ cups/600 ml whole milk

¾ cup/180 ml heavy cream

⅓ cup/75 ml freshly squeezed lemon juice (see box, page 45)

3 Tbsp finely grated lemon zest (see box, page 45)

1 egg, lightly beaten

1 Tbsp unsalted butter

¼ tsp lemon extract

LEMON CURD WHIPPED CREAM

MAKES ABOUT 1 QT/865 G

2 cups/480 ml heavy cream

2 cups/385 g Lemon Curd (recipe follows)

ONE RECIPE LADYFINGERS

(PAGE 54)

Candied lemon peel or yellow sanding sugar for decorating

→

MAKE the PUDDING

In a medium saucepan, combine the granulated sugar, cornstarch, and salt. Add the milk, cream, lemon juice, and lemon zest and whisk to combine. Add the egg, whisk again, and place the saucepan over medium-high heat, whisking constantly.

Once the mixture begins to thicken and bubbles begin popping on the surface, turn the heat to medium and whisk vigorously for 45 seconds. Remove the pan from the heat.

Strain the pudding through a medium-mesh wire sieve into a heatproof bowl. Add the butter and lemon extract and whisk until they are incorporated.

The pudding should be used almost immediately; it should still be warm and relatively pourable when you layer it with the ladyfingers.

MAKE the WHIPPED CREAM

Refrigerate the bowl of a stand mixer and the whisk attachment (or a medium metal bowl and beaters from a hand mixer) until quite cold, about 15 minutes.

Once chilled, remove the bowl and whisk from the refrigerator, add the cream, and whip it on medium speed until just thickened.

Increase the speed to medium-high and whip the cream until it holds stiff peaks that stand upright when the whisk is raised (the stiffer the cream, the more support it will provide the ladyfingers in your cake). Gently fold the lemon curd into the whipped cream, being mindful not to deflate the cream. Use it immediately.

Lightly coat the sides of your springform pan with cooking spray, and line the sides of the pan with a 3-by-29-in/7.5-by-75-cm strip of parchment paper. Using a small offset spatula or the back of a spoon, spread a generous layer of the pudding on the bottom of the pan.

Cover as much of the pudding as possible with a layer of the ladyfingers, filling any gaps with broken ladyfingers. The pieces should touch. The goal is a solid layer of ladyfingers.

Generously spread some of the whipped cream over the ladyfingers.

Continue layering in this order (pudding, ladyfingers, whipped cream, ladyfingers) until you run out or reach the top of the pan. Spread the top of the cake with a final layer of whipped cream and gently cover it with plastic wrap. Refrigerate for 24 hours.

Peel the plastic wrap from the cake and run a paring knife between the paper and the pan. Open the clamp, remove the pan sides, and gently peel back the parchment paper. Transfer the cake, still on the pan bottom, to a serving platter. Sprinkle candied lemon peel or yellow sanding sugar on top of the cake. Using a knife, slice into wedges and serve.

LEMON CURD

In a medium saucepan, lightly whisk together 1 whole egg and 4 egg yolks. Add ¾ cup/ 150 g granulated sugar, ½ cup/120 ml fresh lemon juice, and ¼ cup/20 g fresh lemon zest (see box, page 45) and whisk again. Place the saucepan over medium heat, stirring constantly with a wooden spoon or heatproof spatula, until the curd thickens considerably and your finger leaves a trail on the spoon, 10 to 15 minutes. Do not allow the curd to boil.

Remove the pan from the heat. Strain the curd through a medium-mesh wire sieve into a medium heatproof bowl, using a rubber spatula to push the curd through.

Add 5 Tbsp/70 g unsalted butter and 2 Tbsp heavy cream and whisk until they are incorporated. Place a sheet of plastic wrap over the surface of the curd to prevent a skin from forming and refrigerate until thoroughly chilled, about 2 hours. The lemon curd will keep tightly covered in the refrigerator for up to 5 days.

MAKES ABOUT 2 CUPS/385 G

LEMON-CARAMEL

YIELD: 15 TO 20 SERVINGS

 This cake combines tangy, salty, and sweet in a deliciously tart package.

One 9-by-3-in/23-by-7.5-cm
springform pan

LEMON WAFERS

MAKES ABOUT SIXTY
2¼-IN/5.5-CM WAFERS

2¼ cups/305 g all-purpose flour

½ tsp salt

¼ cup/30 g finely grated
lemon zest (see box, page 45)

1¼ cups/250 g granulated sugar

¾ cup/170 g unsalted butter,
at room temperature

3 Tbsp lemon extract

2 Tbsp freshly squeezed
lemon juice (see box, page 45)

1 Tbsp light corn syrup

EXTRA LEMONY
WHIPPED CREAM

MAKES ABOUT 8 CUPS/1.1 KG

1 qt/960 ml heavy cream

½ cup/65 g confectioners' sugar

¼ cup/60 ml limoncello
(or any lemon-flavored liqueur; optional)

¼ cup/60 ml freshly squeezed
lemon juice (see box, page 45)

¼ cup/20 g finely grated
lemon zest (see box, page 45)

1 tsp lemon extract, or to taste

ONE RECIPE
SALTY CARAMEL

(PAGE 66)

→

MAKE *the* WAFERS

In a medium bowl, whisk together the flour and salt.

In the bowl of a stand mixer, use your fingers to rub the lemon zest into the granulated sugar (this activates the zest and brings out its flavor). Then add the butter and lemon extract and cream them on medium-low speed until slightly fluffy, about 2 minutes. Be careful not to overbeat. Scrape the sides of the bowl with a rubber spatula.

In a small bowl, whisk the lemon juice and corn syrup to combine. Add the juice mixture to the butter-sugar mixture with the mixer on medium-low speed; beat until just combined. Scrape the sides of the bowl with the rubber spatula.

Add the flour mixture all at once to the mixer bowl. With the mixer on low speed, beat until the dough just begins to come together. Scrape the sides of the bowl to fully incorporate all the ingredients.

Divide the dough in half and place each half on a sheet of plastic wrap. Loosely wrap the dough and form each half into a log about 2 in/5 cm wide. Roll the logs along the counter, still wrapped in plastic wrap, in order to shape into perfect cylinders. Tighten the plastic wrap around the logs and freeze them for at least 2 hours, or overnight. If you have trouble forming the soft dough into logs, form the dough into a disk (or loose log shape), wrap it in plastic wrap, and place in the freezer for about 20 minutes, just until it is cold enough to shape into the necessary log. Line two baking sheets with parchment paper.

Once frozen, unwrap one of the logs and use a sharp paring or chef's knife to cut it into thin slices about 1/8 in/3 mm thick; rotate the log as you slice, or the side sitting on the cutting surface will flatten. Arrange the slices about 1 in/2.5 cm apart on one of the prepared baking sheets and place in the freezer for at least 10 minutes. Repeat with the second dough log and prepared baking sheet. If you need more room to fit all your dough slices, simply arrange them on additional sheets of parchment paper, layer the dough-covered papers one on top of the other on the second baking sheet in the freezer, and switch them out as you bake off each batch. (You can also wrap the baking sheets in plastic wrap and freeze the rounds for up to 1 week.)

Position a rack in the center of the oven and preheat to 350°F/180°C.

Place one baking sheet of the frozen dough rounds in the oven and bake until they begin to brown just around the edges, 10 to 12 minutes, rotating the sheet halfway through the baking time. Using a stiff metal or plastic spatula, immediately press down lightly on each cookie to flatten it. Let the wafers cool on the baking sheet for 2 to 3 minutes, then transfer them to a wire rack to cool completely. The wafers should be very crispy when cooled. If they are not, place them back in the 350°F/180°C oven for 1 to 2 minutes more. Repeat to bake the additional sheets of frozen dough rounds.

Store the wafers in an airtight container as soon as they have cooled. They will remain crispy at room temperature, tightly sealed, for about 24 hours. Freezing the baked wafers in a resealable plastic bag also works well, for up to 1 month. There is no need to defrost the wafers before assembling your cake.

MAKE *the* WHIPPED CREAM

Refrigerate the bowl of a stand mixer and the whisk attachment (or a medium metal bowl and beaters from a hand mixer) until quite cold, about 15 minutes.

Once chilled, remove the bowl and whisk from the refrigerator, add the cream, and whip it on medium speed until just thickened.

Add the confectioners' sugar, limoncello (if using), lemon juice, lemon zest, and lemon extract and, on medium-high speed, whip the cream until it holds stiff peaks that stand upright when the whisk is raised (the stiffer the cream, the more support it will provide the wafers in your cake). Use it immediately.

Lightly coat the sides of your springform pan with cooking spray, and line the sides of the pan with a 3-by-29-in/7.5-by-75-cm strip of parchment paper. Using a small offset spatula or the back of a spoon, spread a generous layer of the whipped cream on the bottom of the pan.

Cover as much of the whipped cream as possible with a layer of the wafers, filling any gaps with broken wafers. The pieces should touch. The goal is a solid layer of wafers.

Generously spread a layer of the caramel over the wafers.

Continue layering in this order (whipped cream, wafers, caramel) until you run out or reach the top of the pan. Spread the top of the cake with a final layer of whipped cream and gently cover it with plastic wrap. Refrigerate for 24 hours.

Peel the plastic wrap from the cake and run a paring knife between the paper and the pan. Open the clamp, remove the pan sides, and gently peel back the parchment paper. Transfer the cake, still on the pan bottom, to a serving platter. Using a knife, slice into wedges and serve.

119

STRAWBERRY-LEMON

YIELD: 9 TO 12 SERVINGS

Tart lemons are the perfect foil for sweet strawberries. This light, refreshing, and vibrant-colored cake works especially well in the spring and early summer at the height of strawberry season.

One 8-by-8-by-2-in/20-by-20-by-5-cm square baking pan

ONE RECIPE LEMON PUDDING

(PAGE 112)

LEMON WHIPPED CREAM

MAKES ABOUT 3 CUPS/360 G

1½ cups/360 ml heavy cream

3 Tbsp confectioners' sugar

1½ Tbsp limoncello (or any lemon-flavored liqueur; optional)

1½ Tbsp freshly squeezed lemon juice (see box, page 45)

1½ Tbsp finely grated lemon zest (see box, page 45)

½ tsp lemon extract, or to taste

ONE RECIPE LADYFINGERS

(PAGE 54)

About 3 cups/450 g strawberries, hulled and thinly sliced for layering and decorating

→

MAKE *the* WHIPPED CREAM

Refrigerate the bowl of a stand mixer and the whisk attachment (or a medium metal bowl and beaters from a hand mixer) until quite cold, about 15 minutes.

Once chilled, remove the bowl and whisk from the refrigerator, add the cream, and whip it on medium speed until just thickened.

Add the confectioners' sugar, limoncello (if using), lemon juice, lemon zest, and lemon extract and, on medium-high speed, whip the cream until it holds stiff peaks that stand upright when the whisk is raised. Use it immediately.

Using a small offset spatula or the back of a spoon, spread a generous layer of the pudding on the bottom of the baking pan.

Cover as much of the pudding as possible with a layer of the ladyfingers, filling any gaps with broken ladyfingers. The pieces should touch. The goal is a solid layer of ladyfingers.

Set aside about ¼ cup/40 g of the strawberries for garnish. Layer some of the remaining strawberries over the ladyfingers.

Continue layering in this order (pudding, ladyfingers, strawberries) until you run out or reach the top of the pan. Spread the top of the cake with the whipped cream and gently cover it with plastic wrap. Refrigerate for 24 hours.

Peel the plastic wrap from the cake and scatter the reserved strawberries on top of the cake. Serve portions directly from the pan.

ACKNOWLEDGMENTS

Special thanks from Jean to her mom (a.k.a. Momendorph), who always welcomed her into the kitchen to "cook up a storm" and impressed upon her the importance of using cute vintage tea cups to measure out flour and sugar, provided they were accurate. Also, a pound of the finest chocolate to Michelle Witte, who kept Jean on task during the process and allowed her to continually blur the agent/client line.

Special thanks from Jessie to Matt, of course—her harshest, and therefore most valued, critic. To Matt and Nato, as well, for allowing her to get baked almost every day over these last few years. And to Eric (a.k.a. "Honey Bunny") for helping her squeeze through the kitchen door back in the day and for teaching her so much along the way.

Jean and Jessie would like to thank Amy Treadwell and everyone at Chronicle Books. You are all rock stars with an extra layer of salty caramel!

Thank you (with a cherry on top) to everyone who tested recipes: Kathleen Oliver, Michelle Conrad, Gina Logan Law, Laura Sigman, Janet Sarkos, Kristin Sheehan, Ellen Steinbaum, Amaya Ormazabal, Alex Tart, Amber Oliver, the McGuire Girls, Jennifer Mendelsohn, Lydia Ondrusek, Lucy Savo, Lisa Lynn Bennett, Roanne Kolvenbach, Abigail Landers, Cheryl Bavaro, Nora Martinez DeBenedetto, Gina Hyams, Alyssa Smith, Katie Berkman, Mary Claire Givelber, Bryna Darling, Sherry Cortese, Amy Koltz, John Whiteman, Michelle Charles, Kerry Nolan, and Dawn Frederick.

INDEX

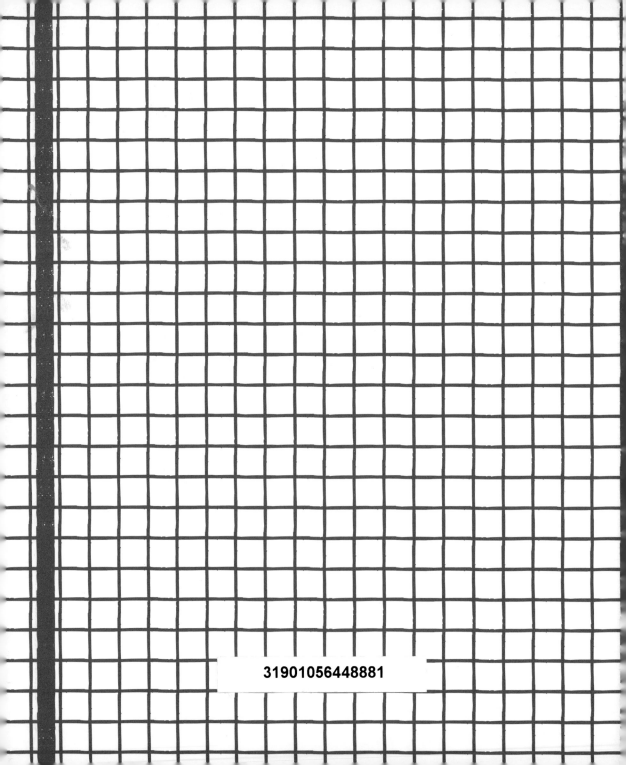

31901056448881